CH00621769

TAX FOR THE SELF-EMPLOYED

TAX FOR THE
SELF-EMPLOYED

David Williams

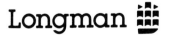

© Allied Dunbar Financial Services Limited 1988

ISBN 0–85121–385–5

Published by

Longman Professional and Business Communications Division
Longman Group UK Limited
21–27 Lamb's Conduit Street, London WC1N 3NJ

Associated Offices

Australia
Longman Professional Publishing (Pty) Limited
130 Phillip Street, Sydney, NSW 2000

Hong Kong
Longman Group (Far East) Limited
Cornwall House, 18th Floor, Taikoo Trading Estate,
Tong Chong Street, Quarry Bay

Malaysia
Longman Malaysia Sdn Bhd
No 3 Jalan Kilang A, Off Jalan Penchala,
Petaling Jaya, Selangor, Malaysia

Singapore
Longman Singapore Publishers (Pte) Ltd
25 First Lok Yang Road, Singapore 2262

USA
Longman Group (USA) Inc
500 North Dearborn Street, Chicago, Illinois 60610

No responsibility for loss occasioned to any person acting or refraining from action as a result of the material in this publication can be accepted by the author or publishers.

The views and opinions of Allied Dunbar may not necessarily coincide with some of the views and opinions expressed in this book which are solely those of the authors and no endorsement of them by Allied Dunbar should be inferred.

The material herein which is Crown copyright is reproduced with the permission of the Controller of Her Majesty's Stationery Office.

A CIP catalogue record for this book is available from the British Library.

Printed in Great Britain by Biddles Ltd, Guildford, Surrey.

David Williams

David Williams is qualified both as a solicitor and a tax
adviser. He has written and lectured widely on both law and
taxation for over a decade. Amongst his other works are
Running your own Business, a companion volume to this,
in the *Allied Dunbar Money Guide* series and practitioners'
and students' books on tax, administrative law and social
security law, as well as other books and regular contributions
to journals and newspapers. He is the consultant editor of
the Reader's Digest guide to the law, **You and your Rights**,
and for several years has appeared on and been a legal adviser
to Granada Television's community advice programme **This
is your Right**. He currently also holds a senior post
sponsored by Price Waterhouse, one of the world's leading
accountancy firms, in the **Centre for Commercial Law
Studies**, Queen Mary College, University of London.

Introduction

1988 has seen the most fundamental changes in taxation for generations, in the same year that our social security system has been radically changed and there has been a thorough shakeout of the systems of grants and incentives for business. If ever one needed an excuse for a book on these subjects, the changes this year *must* provide it. Last year's thinking – on whether your business should be a company; on how to take the profits out of your business; on how to plan for the future; on ways of reducing tax – is out of date. So, to a considerable extent, are last year's books.

Some of last year's attitudes must go fast. Dramatic postures about the levels of tax on business are no longer justified. There is no single rate of tax in the UK over 40%, a point I come back to again and again. If more than half of what you earn goes in tax, that's your fault. Tax is no longer an excuse for not doing things – or for doing things you are better not doing. I know that once upon a time income tax was 98%, but that's not the case now.

Yet for all this, we are paying more tax as a nation than ever before. The need to plan for your business and your future taking tax into account is as strong as ever, as is the need to check you get your full entitlements to allowances, benefits, deductions, grants and incentives.

This book covers all these. It aims to get you started into *every* aspect of tax affecting your business, as well as social security and regional and other grants. It's no good just getting someone to help you with your income tax and expecting the rest to take care of itself. That's another attitude that has to go, along with the attitude that tax is too hard to understand. It isn't. You owe it to yourself to get to grips with all these aspects of taxes, benefits and grants . . . if you don't, you'll only end up owing it to someone else!

Contents

5 Is it an asset?   **55**

1 You and the taxfolk

Ever had one of these?

Inland Revenue

Income Tax (Schedule A or D) and Class 4 National Insurance Contributions

Year 1987-88 ending 5 April 1988

Assessment No.

D_E

In any reply give assessment and/or file no. (if any)

File No.

1 Net amount payable		
	First instalment	**Second instalment**
Income tax	£	£
Class 4 NIC	£	£
Total	£	£

Where tax is payable a notice to pay is attached

Class 4 NIC

Profit	£
Lower limit	£
Charge at % on	£
Amount payable added to	£

Date of issue

SPECIMEN

Notes

General
By law, this notice is addressed to you personally but if you have a professional adviser or agent please let him see this **Notice of assessment** at once.
The enclosed form 64D supplements the notes below.

Estimated assessments
An E before any amount indicates that it has been estimated.

Payment
Payment of any tax and/or Class 4 NIC shown in the **first instalment** box in part 1 above should comply with the directions for payment on the attached **notice to pay** without further request.
Any amount shown in the **Second instalment** box in Part 1 is due on 1 July 1988.
See also note 2 on form 64D.

Appeals and postponement applications
If you disagree with the assessment then appeal in writing within 30 days from the date of issue above. Also, if you consider that the amount charged is excessive you may apply to postpone payment of some or all of the tax etc.
See notes 1 and 2 on form 64D.

Interest on tax payments
Interest is chargeable on tax paid late and may accrue before the amount of tax payable has been agreed.
See note 3 on form 64D.

2 Notice of assessment

Source of profits or income	£	£
Fees est		
Balancing charge		
Deductions Retirement annuity paymts		
Capital allowances		
Class 4 NIC (50%)		
Losses		
Interest, unless paid net of tax		
Allowances		
Personal/Wife's earned income		
Housekeeper/Additional personal		
Dependent relative		
Total allowances		
Less amount allowed in part 3		
Balance given in this assessment		
Net amount chargeable to tax		
Tax chargeable		
Basic rate at % on £		
Higher rate(s) on £		
Additional rate £ at %		
Net tax payable		

I M AITCHISON
HM Inspector of Taxes

(North West 6 District)
St John's House
Merton Road
Bootle
(494) Merseyside L69 9DY

3 Allowances etc allocated

	Allow-ances	Income charged at					
		%	%	%	%	%	%

Is it good news or bad news?

The good news and the bad news

Tax demands are good news and bad news. They are good news if they show you earn a healthy profit from your business, and they ask you to pay the proper amount of tax. Many are bad news, and not just because they demand money. People haven't planned to pay the bill and cannot afford it, or haven't the records to check if they are asked to pay too much, or don't know enough about taxation to know what the bill is about.

Tax is often a big worry to the self-employed and investors living from a combined use of their savings and their skills (as landlords do). It is – and should be – a major concern to those who have a second income from self-employment in addition to the 'day job.' It can be complicated dealing with the competing demands of income tax, capital gains tax, NI contributions, VAT, . . .

The aims of this book

That's where this book comes in. Its purpose is threefold. It is intended to take the unnecessary worry out of tax. It does so by showing you what you need to do to comply with the requirements of the taxfolk, to explain the reasons behind some of the tax rules, and to help you set about planning your tax affairs so you pay no more tax than you should – and no sooner than you should.

Some people respond to the pressures of the tax system by ignoring or evading the taxes. That is increasingly hard to do and the penalties for evading tax are much stiffer than they were – ask anyone caught out for not complying with the VAT laws recently. Others hand their tax affairs over to someone else, without asking any questions. We look at when you may need, and when you may not need help, in the next chapter. Many others just fill in the forms and pay the tax bills without question, assuming the taxfolk must be right. Perhaps they should be, but one survey not long ago found that as many as one in four of all tax computations by the Inland Revenue were wrong! If you do not give them the right information, it is not their fault if they are wrong.

What we do in this book is look at the aspects of your business that are liable to tax (well, let's be honest at the start – *all* aspects of your business are liable to tax, so we will look at all of them). We see what taxes are involved and how to set about handling them. The aims in each case are to show you how the system works, and how to make sure it is working fairly for your business.

Cutting out the jargon

Tax officials and tax advisers love jargon (just like the rest of us!). They'll talk about Schedules and tax points, rollover reliefs and golden handcuffs, categorisation and top-slicing. . . . In this book a determined attempt is made to get the junk element out of what is said. It is impossible to do so entirely, because you need to know some of the jargon, too. To help avoid confusion, there is a list of technical words and jargon at the end of the book, and words defined in that list are put in **bold type** to show that the word is in the list.

On Her Majesty's Service

That's what the envelope says that will bring your tax demands. Of course, Her Majesty is not to blame. Don't forget our tax laws are put in place by the politicians. If you don't like them, don't blame the taxfolk of the Inland Revenue, or Customs and Excise, or the DSS either. It's not their fault that the tax is due. It's the MPs and Her Majesty's Ministers who decided on what shall be levied. It is this (and

previous) governments who are responsible for laying down
the rules that tax officials have to put into effect, and tell
them how to go about it. In this book we try and avoid
taking sides – it is not for us to reason why – but that does
not mean that you should not make your mind up about
what is the good news and what is the bad news. You will
soon know what to do about it! Meanwhile, let us meet the
taxfolk.

Who are the taxfolk?

The Revenue

There are four lots of officials given the job of dealing with
parts of the UK's tax system. The most important group
traditionally are the Commissioners of **Inland Revenue**, or
IRC. The Commissioners are the senior civil servants in
charge of the Inland Revenue Department. There is no
government minister directly in charge of this department,
political control from the Treasury being at a discreet
distance. It is the job of the Inland Revenue to handle income
tax, CGT, corporation tax, inheritance tax, stamp duties and
the valuation of land for business rates. They also help the
DSS collect most NI contributions. IRC staff are divided into
several sections.

You will need to be in touch with your local **Inspector of
Taxes**. Inspectors are those responsible for settling how
much income tax, CGT or corporation tax is payable.
Inspectors are based in local offices throughout the country,
each in charge of a tax **district**. The local office bears the
name of its district – anything from my own tax district
(ominously named 'Tower') to London Provincial 30 (which
is in Stockport). As those two examples show, your local tax
district is not necessarily very 'local', but that is where your
papers will be handled, by the local team of Inspectors,
backed by tax higher executives. Separate from the Inspectors

are the **Collectors of Tax**. These officers (though increasingly these days they seem to be computers!) have the job of checking you pay what is due from you.

Questions about the value of land are dealt with locally by another set of local offices, **District Valuers Offices**. They are responsible not only for land values for capital gains tax and similar purposes, but also in setting ratable values for local rates. Inheritance tax is handled by the **Capital Taxes Office**, and stamp duties by regional **Stamp Duty Offices**, again separate parts of what you can see is a big organisation. The whole operation is run by a central organisation the head office of which is at Somerset House, on the Strand in London.

Customs

The second set of officials you need to contact are the staff of the **Customs and Excise Department**. This is divided between the Waterguard Service and Excise Officers, who deal with customs duty and with the excise duties, and the **VAT Office**, where most businesses have to register for VAT. The VAT headquarters is in Southend, but there are local offices in all parts of the country, and your affairs will be dealt with through your local office.

The 'Social'

Next is the **DSS**, the Department of Social Security. This Department was created just before this book went to print, by splitting the former **DHSS** into two, the other part becoming the (English) Department of Health. These two departments, together with the Scottish and Northern Irish Health Departments, spend over half of all tax collected. The DSS is responsible for collecting NI contributions, and, of course, paying out benefits.

NI contributions and NI benefits are both handled by the

same specialist department in each local Social Security Office – and again there are local Social Security Offices throughout the country. The same local inspectors deal with both contributions and contributory benefits. Contribution matters are dealt with in part by local offices, but many of the issues affecting the self-employed are handled by the Class 4 Group (as it is called) in Newcastle-upon-Tyne.

The Town Hall

Finally, you will get your business rates bill and the community charge levy from the Treasurer's Department of your local council.

Getting in touch

You will be required to provide information to officials of each of these groups at certain times. When and how you do so is set out in the appropriate parts of this book. You will find that the local officials are able to offer you advice about the taxes in their care. All three government departments produce a series of detailed and useful summaries about the taxes they handle, and about particular problems. These are in the form of booklets and leaflets and they are free from local offices – you only need to ask. Again, we give details as we go along.

You will usually find officers will help with advice as well, and help with claims. They clearly cannot run your tax affairs for you, but they may well give you some practical help with points you hadn't thought about. Experience and training have both taught them to view the taxpayer as the 'other side', and most taxpayers treat them in the same way – more so than in some neighbouring countries. So it is worth summarising some of the ground rules on which the taxfolk have to operate.

The authority to tax

The tax departments can only collect tax from you if they have the clear authority of Parliament to do so. Centuries of our constitutional history and several revolutions have (just about) got that established. (If you want to learn something of tax history, borrow a copy of C Northcote Parkinson's *The Law and the Profits* from somewhere – it will tell you all you need to know.) That is of immense practical importance, because it means *they* can only require *you* to pay up if they can show Parliament has ordered you to do so. Before you leap up and down at this ray of hope, be warned – it is safe to say that Parliament has ordered most people to pay tax on most things. But not everything, which is why we need to watch carefully what is and what is not covered.

Basic principles of taxing

The key point is that both you and the tax departments are bound by the rules. From that flow two fundamental principles: that *the tax authorities cannot impose a tax unless the law makes it clear that the tax is properly authorised*, and that *taxpayers cannot escape tax, or ask for deductions, unless they show clear legal authority for that escape or deduction.*

These principles prevent tax authorities operating by whim, but do not avoid disputes – they and you may not agree what the rules say. A third principle applies then – that *you have the right to have disputes decided by impartial judges* in tax tribunals and the courts, though in practical terms it is far better to sort any dispute out by negotiation if you can.

A fourth principle follows from these three – that *you are entitled to conduct your affairs, including your tax affairs, in any way you wish, providing you stay within the law and unless the tax authorities have clear powers to require you to act in one way only.* If you can deal with something in two ways, but one results in you paying less tax – or paying tax later – it is your choice which way you handle the matter. This is called tax avoidance, or tax planning, much of which is just plain common sense.

For the taxfolk's own version of these principles see the Taxpayer's Charter set out on page 10.

'It's too difficult for me to understand'

That's what a lot of people say about their tax affairs, and many of them are wrong. The basic principles of all our taxes are extremely simple. I could summarise the lot on one page. The trouble lies in the detail.

Because of over a century of 'us and them' disputes, the simple frameworks of our taxes have been overlaid by complicated specific provisions dealing with particular problems (frequently overcomplicated and written in some of the worst forms of official English you can find anywhere). The trouble is that our basic principles that there must be clear authority for everything mean that every word of every rule gets pecked and scratched at by tax experts with the same thoroughness that owners of chickens will recognise when their hens are hunting for yet another insect or worm. And, as fowl owners will also know, the result is that what ought to be the vegetable garden gets turned into a mess. The hunt is always on for the foodstuffs to produce a golden egg.

This detail is important in practice, but it should not obscure (as it frequently does) the underlying rules, which are really rather straightforward. It is on those principles, and their practical consequences, that this book concentrates, because that is how the great majority of tax matters are decided. That

is much easier to say since the 1988 Budget has contributed
to a fundamental re-simplifying of our tax systems in much
needed ways. Don't be put off – you *can* understand it.
Then you won't pay too much.

TAXPAYER'S CHARTER
JULY 1986

You have important rights and entitlements as a taxpayer. You are entitled to expect that:

Help and Information

- the staff of the Inland Revenue and Customs and Excise will help you in every reasonable way to obtain your rights and to understand and meet your obligations under the tax laws. So that they can do this, the Inland Revenue and Customs and Excise are entitled to expect that you will give them the full facts they need to decide how much tax you should pay.

Courtesy and Consideration

- the staff of the Inland Revenue and Customs and Excise will at all times carry out their duties courteously, considerately and promptly

Fairness

- you will have your tax liability decided impartially and be required to pay only the amount of tax properly due according to the law
- you will be treated in the same way as other taxpayers in similar circumstances
- you will be presumed to have dealt with your tax affairs honestly, unless there is reason to believe otherwise

Privacy and Confidentiality

- information about your tax affairs which is supplied to the Inland Revenue or Customs and Excise will be treated in strict confidence and used only for purposes allowed by law

Costs of Compliance

- the Inland Revenue and Customs and Excise will have regard to the compliance costs of different taxpayers (including the particular circumstances of smaller businesses). In applying their procedures, they will recognise the need to keep to the minimum necessary the costs you incur in complying with the law, subject to their duty to collect the tax that is due from you efficiently and economically.

Independent Appeal and Review

You may ask the Inland Revenue or Customs and Excise to look again at your case, if you think your tax bill is wrong or they have made a wrong decision, or they have handled your tax affairs badly. Your case can be reviewed by the head of the local office you are dealing with. If you are still not satisfied, you may take the matter up with the Inland Revenue Regional Controller or the Collector of Customs and Excise, or with their Headquarters. Beyond that, you have important rights to independent appeal.

For Inland Revenue taxes, you may appeal against your tax bill to an independent tribunal, the appeal Commissioners, and if necessary to the Courts.

For Customs and Excise taxes and duties, you may appeal against a VAT decision to the independent VAT Tribunals; or in the case of other taxes or duties directly to the Courts.

You may ask your Member of Parliament to take up your case with the office you are dealing with or with Treasury Ministers. Your Member of Parliament may also ask the independent Parliamentary Commissioner for Administration (the Ombudsman) to review your case, if you think that the Inland Revenue or Customs and Excise have handled your tax affairs improperly.

Board of Inland Revenue   **HM Customs and Excise**

2 Don't pay too much

. . . or too little. Set about your tax affairs with the aim of complying with your legal obligations, but at the same time using your rights under the law to pay only the tax which is properly due after all allowances and deductions. Important rules allow you to reduce or postpone – and sometimes entirely to remove – your tax liabilities. The principles we saw in the last chapter mean that it is for you to claim most of these deductions. You won't get them automatically. In this chapter we look at how you set about doing this, including where you may turn for personal advice. First, some 'dos' and 'don'ts'.

Tax 'dos' and tax 'don'ts'

- Do take sensible steps to avoid unnecessary taxation, but don't try to reduce your tax bill by evasion.
- Do find out what deductions you can claim, but don't get carried away into spending money just to save tax.
- Do take tax fully into account when planning your business, but don't let tax considerations dominate all you do.
- Do look to the future for your family and for your own retirement, and don't think it won't happen to you – sooner or later it will.
- Do keep all appropriate books and records for your tax accounts; don't expect the taxfolk to believe you won all your money, or were left it by Great Aunt Agatha unless you have kept the proof.
- Do consider appointing a tax adviser to deal with your tax affairs, but don't use the fact that you have an adviser as an excuse to ignore your tax affairs yourself.
- Do make sure there is a way out of complicated arrangements; don't enter into long term tax saving schemes which might not be completed before the tax rules change.

Do avoid, don't evade

The difference between avoidance and evasion of taxes is fundamental. **Evasion** means cutting tax bills illegally by making sure the taxfolk have never heard of you (**ghosting**), by doing one job on which you are taxed properly whilst keeping quiet about other income (**moonlighting**), or by not passing everything through the till. More crudely, it can involve claiming expenses you never incurred, or even that you are entitled to a married man's allowance when you aren't married. All forms of evasion are illegal and there are stiff penalties awaiting those caught at it. See Chapter 14.

Avoidance means *legally* reducing your tax bills. This involves claiming any deductions, or altering the way you do something to reduce or postpone the tax payable. This is your right within the limits of the law. For instance, anyone who wants to buy a personal pension gets full tax relief on the premium. You are not required, as a self-employed person, to do this, but if you do, the Government in effect, will pay part of the cost. Some kinds of avoidance aren't there deliberately, but because of history, or a mistake. Why they are there does not matter to you – either way, if you take the right steps, you pay less.

Do plan and do comply

There should be two stages to your handling of tax matters. The first is tax **planning**. This is taking tax into account when planning what to do, and looking at things **post-tax**, that is, after tax has been paid and allowances granted. In my book *Running your own business* (also published by *Longman*, as part of the *Allied Dunbar Money Guide* series) I urge readers to 'Plan the 5 Ps'—purpose, products, potential, people, pounds. In each case, there is some aspect of your planning that may be affected by tax, sometimes quite sharply. I repeat here what I say there – plan it!

The tail should not wag the dog. Do not be one of those who devise everything just so as not to pay tax. There is no point investing in some useless machine just because the cost is tax-deductible; or in setting up some complicated arrangement which totally changes the way the business runs just to save some cash.

The top rate is 40%

When the top rate of income tax was 98% (and it is only ten years ago since that was so!) and the top rate of death duties was 80% (and that's quite recently, too) and the top rate of tax on gains from land was going to be a straight 100% (yep – the lot!) people went to great lengths to avoid these rates.

Since 1988, things are radically different. *There is now no single rate of tax over 40%*, whether income tax, capital gains tax, corporation tax, NI, VAT or death duties.

Avoiding avoidance

At the same time, the most artificial of the dodges people used when tax rates were much higher have now been stopped – either by the courts or in Parliament – by **anti-avoidance** measures. These are rules designed expressly to stop people avoiding tax. They simply stop you not paying, and mean your plans to sidestep have been a waste of time and money. Their effect must be watched, but it is limited in most cases to stopping 'clever' avoidance tricks, where people do things not for a proper commercial reason, but only, or mainly, to reduce tax. If you think you have spotted a clever wheeze to avoid tax, you may be right (and, like other people, you probably won't shout about it if you find it works), but if

what you are doing is purely to avoid tax, don't be surprised
if the taxfolk have got there first.

The other stage besides planning is what the professionals call
tax **compliance** – making sure you have met your legal
obligations by registering with the tax authorities, making
returns to them, and paying tax bills. Your business needs
to meet the separate requirements of each tax, because the
rules for each tax are different, as are the officials handling
them.

What taxes matter to *me*?

You will be involved, as an unpaid collector of taxes, with
several taxes. The best way to summarise what you need to
watch is by referring to different kinds of income or
transactions:

- *Trading income* – this is taxed in three ways at once:
  — there is an income tax charge on your **net profits** from
    the trade, that is, on the income less the expenses.
    This is called **Schedule D Case I** (its official name in
    tax law).
  — there is an NI contributions charge on the net profits,
    backed by a flat rate levy on all the self-employed.
  — there is value added tax (VAT) on each VATable
    supply of goods or services made by the trade.
  If the trade is run by a company, it will not pay income
  tax. Instead it pays corporation tax on the profits.
  Companies do not pay NI contributions except for their
  employees.
- *Professional income* – tax, eg, on architects and doctors,
  is levied in the same three ways as trading income, but
  is called **Schedule D Case II**.
- *Gains from selling capital items* – selling capital items
  used in a business (eg a shop or land) is treated the same
  way for tax purposes as private sales (such as a valuable

painting). In either case, the individual may be liable for
a capital gains tax charge on the profits from the sale. A
company making a gain does not pay CGT, but a charge
to corporation tax on a chargeable gain; unless your main
business activity is selling such items and then it could
be charged to income tax. If the seller is in business, he,
she or it will also probably have to charge VAT on
making the sale. And if selling land or shares, you will
be caught by a third tax, **stamp duty** although VAT is
not charged on land sales.

- *Exports and imports* – whilst profits on exports and
imports are treated the same for income tax purposes as
goods bought or sold in the UK, the VAT rules are
entirely different. If you are exporting goods to a country
outside the European Community, or importing goods
from outside, you must watch **customs duties** when the
goods are imported.

- *Income from overseas* – this is dealt with by separate
rules from those applying to income from inside the UK
(and covered by **Schedule D Cases IV and V**) If you
have little connection with the UK, there will be no, or
only a reduced, liability to tax. This book concentrates
(as do most others) on the rules that operate here, so
this is an extra reason to seek advice.

- *Rents, etc, from land* – landlords pay income tax on rents
from land under a different set of rules to those applying
to trading income, known as **Schedule A**. NI
contributions do not apply to a landlord's income from
land. VAT is not usually payable on rent.

- *Using land* – whilst it might sound odd to be taxed on
using land, that is how the **business rates** work. It is
assumed that you are paying rent on your land (even if
you are not), and the amount of rates is based on this
rent.

- *Dividends from companies* – individuals receiving
dividends and other distributions from companies in the
UK pay income tax on them – though the company has
invariably paid this for you. The income tax rules for
this again differ from trading income rules and are known

as **Schedule F**. Companies receiving these payments do not pay any further tax. There is no VAT on dividends.

- **Interest** – the rules for taxing interest are rather messy, but normally with long term loans income tax (or, in the case of companies, corporation tax) is payable under yet another set of rules, **Schedule D Case III**.

  Yet other rules apply to some forms of government stock, and some forms (like National Savings) are not liable to tax at all. VAT is not charged on interest.

- **Earnings from employment** – these are liable to two taxes:
  — income tax under yet another set of income tax rules (**Schedule E**), and
  — NI contributions payable both by employee and employer.

- **Pensions** – whether paid by the employer, the state, or personal pension or private scheme, these are treated in the same way as earnings. Some social security payments, like retirement pensions, are liable to tax, – others are not.

- **Prizes and winnings** – most prizes and winnings are free of tax (except the special taxes on betting, football pools and so forth). Prizes won from professional competitions may be treated as professional or trading income.

- **Gifts and bequests** – these do not get caught by income tax (unless they are a disguised form of earnings). They may get caught for:
  — capital gains tax as if there had been a sale (this can be postponed, as shown below). There is no CGT payable when someone leaves property to someone else on death;
  — inheritance tax, if the gift is large and occurs within seven years of the giver's death.

- **Grants** – most grants are liable to income tax, though some are tax free. Grants from private sources are sometimes treated as gifts or prizes.

- **Increased value of unsold items** – the fact that your assets, such as the business used for your business, go up in value during the year has no effect on your tax position. We have no **wealth tax** on property you own. The one exception to this is **trading stock**. The value of trading stock is taken into account in working out trading profits for income tax or corporation tax.

So, what taxes are involved?

You may find it useful to have that information summarised tax by tax. In most cases, you need to think about – and probably pay – the following:

Income tax – on trading profits, rents, professional income, bank interest, dividends, other savings interest and earnings from employment.

Business rate – on all business premises, payable to the local council.

Capital gains tax (almost always called **CGT**) – on any gain you make when disposing (whether by sale, exchange gift or otherwise) of any kind of property, but where the gain is not regarded as trading income.

Community charge (also called poll tax) – will be payable by all individuals to the councils of the areas where they live. It replaces the domestic rates on private houses.

Corporation tax – paid by companies instead of income tax and CGT; its rules are much the same as IT and CGT.

Customs duty – on any goods you import from outside the **Common Market**, but not on items you get, say, from France. Similarly, if you export to countries outside the Common Market, your goods will probably be subject to customs duty as they enter the importing country.

Inheritance tax (IHT) – is really two taxes in one – a tax on property left by someone at death, and a tax on gifts made within seven years before death. It only affects large sums, but is important in long term planning.

NI contributions – all self-employed people, like all employees must pay NI contributions out of their earnings.

Stamp duty – payable when you buy or lease land or buy shares or stock. It is a levy on the value of the land or shares changing hands.

Value added tax (called, here as everywhere else, VAT) – tax on all supplies of goods and services made by businesses.

These aren't all the UK taxes. There are **excise duties** levied on tobacco, petrol, beer, wine and spirits, even a gas levy, which have to be paid. Costly as these are, they are specific taxes paid by producers or importers, or by those needing licences to keep, say, gaming machines or guns. These are mentioned where appropriate in the book. There are also other taxes, such as petroleum revenue tax, which we ignore because they won't affect your business (unless you are in the oil industry).

What to do when starting

Notify the tax authorities in the right way when your business starts, and when you start employing someone. Here's a checklist of who you must tell and when:

Checklist: Notifying the tax authorities

- The *Inspector of Taxes* for your district (find out your local district from the phone book under 'Inland Revenue'). The Inspector must be notified when you take on a member of staff who will earn more than about £45 a week, so you operate the PAYE system on the employee's pay. The Inspector must also be told when you start your business, so that returns can be sent to sort out any income tax due. You can give this notification on Form 41G. There is a copy of this at the back of the book. If the business is run by a company, a slightly different form, CT 41G, is needed. If you were previously working for someone else, you should also send your P45 (given you by your last employer) to the Inspector.

- The *VAT Office* for your area (find the address from your phone book under 'Customs and Excise'). You must notify them as soon as you are liable to register for VAT (see Chapter 4). This you do on Form VAT 1. There is a copy of this at the back of the book.

- Your local *Social Security Office* (find out where by looking in the phone book under 'Health and Social Security, Dept of'). You must notify them if you are employing anyone, so you collect NI contributions owed by them (and you). Notify the DSS so that they can sort out your own liability to contributions, even if your earnings are low enough for you not to have to pay. Use Form CF 11 if you are becoming self-employed and will pay contributions, but Form CF 10 if you think you are entitled not to pay weekly contributions. There are copies of these at the back of the book. There is another form, Form CF 351, available in leaflet NI 255 from Social Security Offices or Post Offices which allows you to pay contributions by direct debit.

Helping yourself

Your main task, in getting to grips with taxation, is to make sure you keep proper books and records so you can keep the taxfolk satisfied about the information you give them. Advice on record-keeping is given in *Running your own business (Longman)*. Each tax requires different information to be recorded, and the rules for VAT, PAYE and NICs are strict.

The other task is to think through what you do to see if you could do it better from a tax point of view, for example paying employees partly in kind so as to avoid income tax and NICs.

You will find plenty of experts prepared to help you do either of these things – at a price. Is it a price worth paying?

Professional advice

The vast majority of small businesses employ an **accountant**
to 'do the books'. Most get their accountants to do their tax
affairs as well. That can be both good and bad. Most
accountants help with both tax compliance and tax planning.
They often earn their fees back and more, with the tax they
save as a result.

At the other end there are, sadly, quite a number of
incompetent 'advisers' about, and you need to beware of
them. They are trading on your (and, often, their own)
ignorance. Because of the requirements of secrecy on
government officials, they have quite an easy life. You don't
know, do you, whether the tax they say you have to pay is
more or less than it should be? What is more, if the accountant
gets things wrong, he can usually put the blame on the tax
authorities – it's *their* fault that you've suddenly been
confronted with a large tax bill. But is it? Rather too many
taxpayers are ready to assume it is, even though they don't
know.

Of course, tax officials make mistakes, but I know from
experience that some accountants make them too, without their
clients realising it. This is hardly surprising, because anyone
can set up in business as a 'tax accountant' without having
passed a single examination in anything, or indeed knowing
anything at all about our tax system. Some Tax Inspectors
have blacklists of local firms they don't like, but you won't
find out who's on it. What you can – and should – do is check
the firm you choose consists of professionally qualified people
and has a good reputation. And find something out about the
tax system yourself, so you know what to expect.

Do I have to appoint a tax accountant?

No. The Revenue often prefer it (provided the person you appoint is not on the blacklist) because it often makes life easier for them. The only thing that can be required is information. In a small business, you may be able to handle this yourself. Some people are happy to get an accountant to help them for a few years to set up a pattern which they can then follow themselves.

If bringing in an expert, make sure he or she is just that. One way is to check her or his professional qualifications. The best will be members of professional institutes, particularly **Chartered Accountants** and **Certified Accountants**. There are details about this in *Running your own business*.

Help from solicitors

Besides accountants, two other professions can help with compliance work or planning work. All **solicitors** are trained in tax affairs, and may prove particularly useful in dealing with company taxation. Not all solicitors deal, or should deal, with tax matters, so, again, check up on whether a firm deals with much tax work, and on its local reputation.

The Institute of Taxation

There is one specialist body just for tax, the **Institute of Taxation**. Its members are tax practitioners who have passed specialist examinations in tax. Many of its members are also qualified accountants or solicitors, but some are tax advisers with this qualification alone. They use the initials **FTII** or

ATII. Like solicitors and chartered or certified accountants, you have some guide to competence when they are employed.

Other sources of help

Banks and other financial businesses will also help. Advice about any kind of tax saving proposals, such as leasing schemes or savings, is usually readily available from those who supply the schemes and products. If thinking about any of these aspects, shop around. There is also help available from the taxfolk themselves, both in the form of leaflets and guides, and individual advice on particular queries. I know more than one person who went along to the taxfolk to get help with some tax problem, and came away with some useful tips on tax-saving that weren't expected!

The globe-trotting taxpayer

One way of avoiding UK taxes is to leave the UK. Sounds obvious and simple, but again it was not easy for many people until 1979. By 1992, on present plans, the 12 states of the Common Market will be just that – a common market open to all. But anything happening outside the UK is likely to involve foreign tax. Not always because there are tax havens where there is no or little tax. For example, the Cayman Islands do not have a tax system (instead, I am told, you get eaten alive by the mosquitos – you can't have everything!). Throughout the European Communities (EC) and most other states, taxes are similar to ours. But if you have connections with another state, or you start to do business outside the UK, you will probably end up with a **double taxation** problem – paying tax in two places on the same transactions or profits. If thinking of expanding overseas, or you have strong foreign connections, get expert advice at the beginning from someone who knows the overseas position.

3 A tax on your profits

You must pay both income tax and NICs on your trading or professional profits. If you have income of any other kind (see the list in Chapter 2), you will pay income tax but not NICs on it, though the rules are different. In practice, the Revenue let you put small amounts of other income (eg rent for subletting a room in the office) into the business accounts, but where you have two incomes – as when someone is both self-employed and an employee – they must be kept separate. This is because different rules apply to each kind of income. In this chapter we look at how income tax works, and at rules for taxing trading income. Rules applying only to companies are dealt with in Chapter 6.

How income tax works

Income tax is an annual tax, that is, it is a tax on the total income of all kinds you receive each year. The rules require that each year all the taxable kinds of income you receive are totalled up. You are allowed some deductions from that total, such as a **personal allowance** and **interest relief**. The balance left is your **taxable income** for the year, on which income tax is due.

Tax rates are reviewed every year. The present Government, like governments in many countries, is committed to reducing income tax rates. The current rates are set out in the box opposite, along with the main allowances.

The income tax rates and allowances for 1988–89

Basic rate of income tax **25%**
Higher rate of income tax **40%**
(The higher rate is payable on each £1 of income,
once the total *taxable* income of the taxpayer
exceeds £19,300.)

Single personal allowance **£2,605**
(Wife's earnings relief is the same)
Married personal allowance **£4,095**
(A single parent also gets this allowance)
Higher amounts are payable to those over retirement age and the
blind.

The income tax year

In the box on income tax rates we mention **1988–89**. This
refers to the **income tax year** starting in 1988. This starts
on **6 April**) each year. Why? Because it did last year . . . and
that's what they said last year too. However, if we look back
far enough we can blame the shift in the Gregorian calendar
as the cause for the tax year now being a few days after a
Quarter Day, although the whole story is more complicated
than we need to examine here. The Government's financial
year (and the tax year for companies and for most taxes) starts
appropriately on All Fools Day, **1 April**. Because the income
tax year straddles two calendar years – it runs through to 5
April the following year – the abbreviation 1988–89 is used
to refer to an income tax year. For companies, the reference
is different. The **Financial Year 1988** means the corporation
tax year starting on 1 April 1988, and running to 31 March
1989.

How much income tax do I pay?

The total income tax payable depends on your total income and allowances for the income tax year. For example, suppose you earn in total £20,000 in 1988–89, and you are single, then you are entitled to a personal allowance of £2,605. (You can earn this much before paying any tax.) So you have £17,395 (£20,000 less £2,605) taxable pay, taxed at 25%. Your tax bill will be £4,349, if you have no other deductions. It's worth noting that the *average* rate of tax you pay is about 22% (the total tax divided by the total income).

Everyone is entitled to a personal allowance, single or married. People over retirement age (65 for men, 60 for women) are entitled to higher allowances, with more again at 80.

Husbands and wives

A married man living with his wife is covered by a peculiar set of rules to be abolished in 1990 (about a century late), but which until then regard her income as part of his income – even if the wife is self-employed in her own name! The husband is charged income tax on the total of all income of both of them. If the wife is working he (not she!) is entitled to an extra allowance, called the **wife's earned income relief**, as well as the married personal allowance. He gets this even if he does not work, but only gets it if his wife has earnings. The moral of this is that if the husband is running his own business, and his wife is not working, she ought to do some work for him, so that he can pay her a maximum of just less than the wife's earned income relief (about £2,600 in 1988–89). See Chapter 8.

On what income do I pay?

Income tax is based on the total of all kinds of income *taxable* in that year. That does not mean the income is either *earned* or *received* in that year. For most kinds of income (such as interest, dividends and earnings) that is true, but not for trading income. There the rules are in part set by you – it depends on what your accounts year is.

Trading accounts years and tax years

Income tax on trades is generally charged on a **preceding year basis**. The amount of profits taxed in any one year is based on the amount of profits made by you in *your accounts year which ended in the preceding tax year*. For example, if you run your accounts on a calendar year basis, the accounts end on 31 December. The accounts on which your tax bill will be based in 1988–89 are therefore *not* the accounts for 1988 and 1989, but the accounts year which ended in 1987–88. This will be the accounts for the year ending 31 December, 1987.

Because of this rule it pays to choose when you start your accounts year carefully. If you run your accounts on a tax year basis, you pay tax on your income for the year ending 5 April 1988 in the tax year 1988–89, about 12 months later. If you run your accounts on an accounts year running from 1 May to 30 April you pay tax on your income for the year ending 30 April 1988 in the tax year 1989–90, a whole year later.

Accounts in the first few years

These 'preceding year' rules do not work for the first few years of a trade, so special rules apply. In the **first** year, tax is paid on the actual profits of the year to 6 April (usually rounded to 31 March). In the **second** year, tax is paid on the profits of the first 12 months of the business. In the **third** year, tax is paid on the usual basis (ie the accounts year ending in the second year – but this is the first 12 months again!).

The taxpayer (*not* the Revenue) can choose to be taxed on the actual profits of the second and third years, as well as the first year, if that helps. A careful bit of planning should make that choice unimportant. You should, for tax reasons, aim *not* to make a large profit in your first year. You probably won't anyway in many businesses, because of all the up-front expenses when the business starts. Let's see how this works.

EXAMPLE

Al starts up in business on 1 May 1988. There are a lot of expenses in the first few months, and Al makes a small loss of £1,200. (Maybe this was helped a little by forgetting to ask a major creditor to pay a bill for £2,400 until after 1 May 1989, but the books weren't fiddled.) What will Al pay?

Tax year:	Profits taxable:	Amount:
1988–89	To 6 April 1989	NIL
1989–90	First 12 months	NIL
1990–91	Accounts to 30.4.89	NIL

Try re-working those figures assuming Al had made a profit of £1,200 in the first year. How much tax would have been paid by 1991?

For special rules for closing years, see Chapter 12.

Accounts and tax

Income tax trading rules take account of the accounts year of the business. How far are they based on the accounts themselves? That is the subject of the rest of this chapter, and the next two chapters. We shall see that the answer is: partly. To give some idea of the problems, a simple set of profit and loss accounts are set out on the next pages to indicate points to be watched.

As the model accounts suggest, the basic rule is that ordinary commercial accounts cannot be used without adjustment as tax accounts. This is so even though the accounts have been audited and an auditor has certified them as 'true and fair' under the Companies Acts.

Trading profits: the basic rules

In calculating the profits of a business in any year for income tax purposes, what are needed are the following figures, which are taken, after adjustment, from the trading accounts:

- the total income from the business for the year (excluding any capital sums received)
- the total allowable expenditure of the year in running the business
- the opening stocks of materials or inventory at the start of the year
- the closing stocks at the end, valued in the same way as the opening stocks.

How accounts should be adjusted for tax reasons

FAVOURED FLOGGLES

If you make all the adjustments necessary and desirable to these accounts, what is FF's taxable profit? You will find it is rather different to the loss claimed!

Profit and loss account for the year ending 31 March 19**[1]

	£	£
Turnover		60,000 [2]
Cost of sales:		
Opening stock	2,000 [3]	
Purchases	32,000	
	34,000	
less closing stock	4,000 [3]	
		(30,000)
Gross profit		30,000
add rental income		1,000 [4]
		31,000
Expenses:		
Staff pay	15,000	
Own and staff NI	2,000 [5]	
Rent and rates	2,500	
Heat and light	300	
Telephone	500 [6]	
Repairs and improvements	1,200 [7]	

[1] Why end the year then – why not 30 April?

[2] Assuming most supplies are standard-rated, Fab should be registered for VAT. If so, all VAT should be left out of these accounts.

[3] Opening and closing stock must be valued on the same basis.

[4] Rental income should strictly be dealt with separately.

[5] Class 1 and *half* Class 4 contributions are deductible, but *not* Class 2.

[6] Does this include personal calls? They are not allowable.

[7] Repairs can be deducted, but *not* improvements.

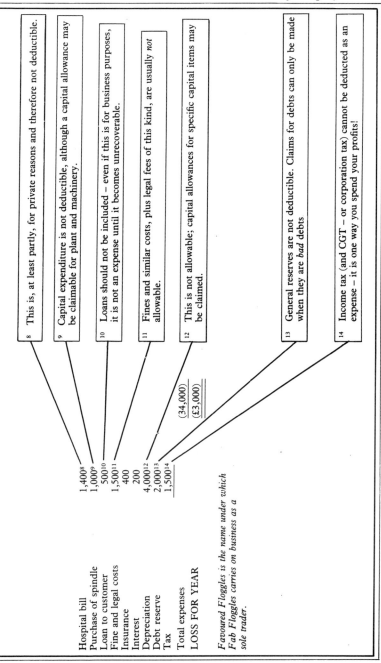

8 This is, at least partly, for private reasons and therefore not deductible.

9 Capital expenditure is not deductible, although a capital allowance may be claimable for plant and machinery.

10 Loans should not be included – even if this is for business purposes, it is not an expense until it becomes unrecoverable.

11 Fines and similar costs, plus legal fees of this kind, are usually *not* allowable.

12 This is not allowable; capital allowances for specific capital items may be claimed.

13 General reserves are not deductible. Claims for debts can only be made when they are *bad* debts

14 Income tax (and CGT – or corporation tax) cannot be deducted as an expense – it is one way you spend your profits!

Hospital bill	1,400[8]
Purchase of spindle	1,000[9]
Loan to customer	500[10]
Fine and legal costs	1,500[11]
Insurance	400
Interest	200
Depreciation	4,000[12]
Debt reserve	2,000[13]
Tax	1,500[14]
Total expenses	(34,000)
LOSS FOR YEAR	(£3,000)

Favoured Floggles is the name under which Fab Floggles carries on business as a sole trader.

Capital allowances and other adjustments will then be made to the taxable profits.

> **Taxable profits =   Income**
> **+ Closing stock**
> **− Expenses**
> **− Opening stock**

Cash or earnings

Should the accounts show what the business has earned, or what cash it has received during the year? There may be a considerable difference between these figures. The Revenue usually insist, after the business has got going, that accounts are on an **earnings basis,** that is, the accounts show what has been earned even if it has not been paid for. This means that, for example, an item should be regarded as sold, or a service as completed, when the bill is sent out rather than when it is paid. The rule is similar to the main rule for VAT (though smaller businesses have recently been allowed to swap to cash accounting for VAT in many cases).

This rule makes it harder to play around with accounts for tax purposes (which is why it is the rule). However, it may still be worthwhile speeding up or slowing down the issue of bills near the end of a year. For example, if your earnings are just going to tip you into the 40% rate, it may be better to wait than get them a month earlier and pay 15% more tax on them. Alternatively if you have a major deduction to declare, reducing your taxable income sharply that year, it may be better to collect bills in faster.

Bad debts

The problem with the earnings rule is that, inevitably, not everyone pays up. You become liable to pay tax when you send out the bill, but you may never be paid if the debtor becomes insolvent. Most wiser businessmen take that into account and have a bad debts reserve. Maybe, but the tax authorities won't wear that. You can deduct unpaid debts only when they become bad debts, that is, they are not reasonably collectable.

Your own debts

The same rule works in reverse on the bills incurred by the business. These should go into the accounts when the bills are incurred, rather than when the business pays them. Again, the speed of incurring debts can be accelerated or decelerated near the end of the accounts year if there seems good reason to do so.

Trading income

Two issues need to be sorted out in deciding whether a sum is to be included as income in the profit and loss accounts of a business. First, is the sum income from that trade or profession or is it received for some other reason? That raises two questions – when is something *from* the business, and what is the meaning of **trade** and **profession**? Sums received from other sources, such as rent, have to be taxed under other rules. Exceptionally, the sum may not be taxable at all but may, for example, be a gift to the trader (as there is no income tax on genuine personal gifts). Gifts of this sort are unusual and arise only where a trader has no contractual right to, or expectation of, the payment, and it is made either with a customer who has ceased trading with the trader or someone who is not a customer. They might take the form of a prize, such as a literary prize given to someone not just for the exercise of their professional skills, but for something out of the ordinary. Or they may be a gift left by someone in a will, for example, to their hairdresser or doctor.

What are trades and professions?

The precise words in law are 'trade', 'profession' and 'vocation', but it matters little whether something is described as one or the other. Just two points should be watched:

- **Self-supply** – if you use your own trading stock, you must treat the supply as a sale, and put it in the accounts. If you supply yourself with services, eg doctors diagnosing themselves or a carpenter repairing the family furniture, you do not have to account for the time spent. Otherwise lawyers' tax bills might be much larger!
- **One-offs** – you can be trading even though you only buy and sell something once. But you don't become a journalist by writing one article for the newspapers. One-off items such as that are still taxable, but under different rules which have the effect of charging the sums separately for the year in which they are received (called **Schedule D Case VI** in the tax laws).

There is no tidy definition of a **trade**. It includes any kind of manufacturing, importing or creating goods, selling, hiring or lending, or providing services of any kind (except those that would be called professional). The fact that the trade is illegal or unique is irrelevant. It matters only that it is the sort of thing people do for a profit.

Professions are those activities which rely on personal intellectual skills, and is a rather snobbish tax rule. Lawyers are professionals and stockbrokers are not. Selling photographs might be a profession, but selling cameras is not.

The key common element 'o trades and professions is that they involve the direct earning of the profits with some offsetting revenue expenditure. They are separate from the activity of a landlord who earns money by letting his property at a rent (though a landlord who provides services at the same time as the 'let', eg holiday homes where trips and facilities such as water-skiing are provided for those staying, would also be a trader).

Income or capital?

Deciding whether something is income (which must go in the profit and loss account) or capital (which does not, but is taxable by CGT) is a more usual problem, and has caused many disputes between the Revenue and taxpayers in the past. The chief reason for the disputes was that whilst the rates of income tax were anything from 30% to 98%, there was no tax on capital profits until the 1960s, and then the maximum rate was 30% in all cases.

The change in 1988

The 1988 Budget was revolutionary in removing, for the first time ever, the difference in rates between income profits and capital profits. Generations of tax experts have been trained into the finer arts of distinguishing income from capital. In most cases it now hardly matters which it is. It will rarely be worth trying to turn what is really income into capital – the aim of many tax avoidance schemes over the years. Nor will it make any difference for VAT purposes. One difference – that NI contributions are payable on income but not on capital receipts – does not apply when total income exceeds about £15,000.

Although, therefore, it will rarely be worth quarrelling too long about the finer aspects of the divide any longer, the divide is still of importance for accounting purposes. Its other likely importance for tax purposes is in claiming relief if a loss is made. The rules allowing relief for income losses are much more generous than those for capital losses (see Chapter 4).

The line is one between profits from a trading-style transaction, and the sale of an investment or of part of the permanent capital base of a business. This is sometimes called the *circulating* capital of the business as against the *fixed* capital. In borderline cases, the taxfolk look at such things as the length of time the item has been held before sale, how many times items like that have been sold by the trader, the reason for sale, and the kind of items sold (stocks and shares are usually investments, and paintings and furniture often are, but people rarely buy 1000 crates of baked beans as an investment or for personal use).

Expenses

What expenditure is, and what is not, allowable against trading income is dealt with in the next chapter. Allowances for capital expenses are dealt with in Chapter 5.

Trading stock

The final element in fixing the trading profit or loss for a year is to take account of the **trading stock**. This means the stock of items held at the beginning and end of each year for sale by or use in the business. In the case of a service industry which is providing services rather than goods, account also needs to be taken of **work in progress**, that is, the value of outstanding work done and to be done under contracts for which bills have not yet been prepared.

It is important to take account of trading stock and work in progress in working out the true profit of a business. It will be rare for a business to finish the year with the same level of stocks as at the start. However, the business will use its profits to buy new stock, and equally can save money by running down its stocks. Unless stock figures are taken into account, the cash figures of profit may be too high or too low.

Valuing the stock

The Revenue requires tax accounts to contain valuations for stock and work in progress at the beginning and end of each year. How should this be valued? In many trades there are well-established ways of valuing stock, and use of these will be accepted by the Revenue. Apart from such methods, the Revenue cannot insist on any one method of stock valuation, provided that the method used is a fair one used consistently, and which over time reveals the full profits of the business. It is not acceptable to change methods during the year in the hope of losing some profit. That the Revenue will correct.

One widely used method is to value the stock at the lower of cost of buying the stock, and current market value. On most stock this means holding the stock at its purchase value; but where stock has deteriorated or gone out of fashion, it can be written down to what it is likely to fetch when sold. This is the guide widely accepted by the accountancy profession, and laid down in one of its Statements of Standard Accountancy Practice.

4 Expenses you can claim

It is vital, if you are not to pay too much tax or VAT, that you keep notes of your business expenses, and set against your profits all expenses you incur that you are entitled to deduct.

Income tax on a business is based on the **net profits** after taking into account all allowable expenses. NI contributions on the self-employed are based in part on the income tax accounts, so also take expenses into account. Equally, liability to CGT depends on the gain made, not total sales proceeds. VAT is based on tax collected less tax paid out so, again, expenses need to be taken fully into account.

Unfortunately, but not surprisingly, there are rules which determine what expenses are allowable as deductions and what are not. In some cases you are allowed only part of your expense as a deduction, in other cases none at all. This chapter examines (in alphabetical order) many kinds of expense you may make, to see the tax position. Before we do this, some general points need to be noted.

The real cost of expenses

When looking at business expenses, do not look at what you pay out but at the real cost of your expense after your taxes are paid – the post-tax position. The following example of Zale's carpets shows the difference.

EXAMPLE

What's does it cost *after* tax?

Zale, who is VAT registered and pays income tax and Class 4 NICs, decides to buy for £1,000 a new carpet for work and also, for another £1,000, a new carpet for the sitting room at home.

Carpets are taxed to VAT at the standard 15% (rates correct at the time of writing), so the true price of both carpets is £870 plus VAT of £130. Zale can claim back the £130 VAT on the business carpet against the output tax but cannot get back the VAT on the sitting room carpet.

The work carpet therefore costs £870 after VAT. Zale can also claim an income tax deduction for the carpet, by way of capital allowances (see Chapter 5) which will over time allow a full deduction of the cost of the carpet. The same thing will automatically happen for Class 4 contributions. Although not immediately, Zale gets the full cost of the carpet set off against profits, saving income tax at 25% (it might be 40%) and NICs at 6.3% (though, if tax is 40%, there will be no NIC), a total of 31.3% off the £870 (£272). The true cost of this carpet is therefore £668, or two-thirds of the full-cost sitting room carpet. Still not cheap, but it does make a difference!

Keep proper records

Of course, Zale cannot just make up the fact that the new work carpet was purchased. A new carpet must actually be bought. To show the taxfolk that expenses are properly claimed, you need effective records of what you spent, and when you spent it, as part of your accounts. This is particularly important for VAT.

General rules for each tax

Income tax on profits – To be allowed, an expense must be:

- of an income or revenue, not capital, nature

- wholly and exclusively spent on the business
- not expressly disallowed by law.

Expenses allowable to a landowner against rent are covered in Chapter 11. No expenses are allowed to individuals for expenses in connection with investments and savings (such as shares or bank interest).

Capital gains tax – To be allowed, the expense must be a capital (not income or revenue) expense incurred on the item being disposed of, and of one of the kinds expressly allowed by law (see also Chapter 5).

VAT – To be allowed as *input tax*, the VAT must have been paid on goods or services used for business purposes, and not expressly disallowed by law (see Chapter 10).

Trying it on

The income tax rule that expenses must have been 'wholly and exclusively' for the business is a strict one. It was designed to stop purely private expenses being set off against business profits. But, strictly, it also prevents expenses made partly for the business and partly private being set off as well. For example, the clothes you wear for work, unless they are a uniform or protective clothing, will be regarded partly as worn for work but also partly to keep you decent and warm, and so not deductible. And if you use your telephone both for work and private use, the rental will not strictly be allowable.

In practice the Revenue do not usually insist on this attitude on most expenses. They will agree a reasonable split for, say, a telephone bill or car expenses, as we note below. But if you try pushing your luck too hard, they may in turn claim to apply the law strictly – when you will lose out.

How the Revenue check

The Revenue approach to business accounts is necessarily somewhat selective. What they want are properly prepared accounts. In most cases, after a simple check for arithmetic, they will be accepted. If not satisfied (and in some random cases) they will ask for further evidence from your books and invoices. They can also make other checks on a statistical basis.

One thing they watch is the mark-up of the business. They have available to them not just the accounts of your business, but those of all your rivals. If they find that, say, one fish and chip shop seems to have heavy expenses and is only making 10% profit, whilst all the other in the area are making 30%, they will rightly be suspicious until they have some evidence to prove this heavy expenditure. (More seriously, they may also suspect that income is being understated, and investigate that, too.) They also have powers to check with the VAT people about VAT returns. If the tax and VAT returns are found to be different, someone has some explaining to do!

56 kinds of expense

Note: under each head we look at the income tax (IT) rules, then any special VAT rules (after VAT) any special Capital Gains Tax (CGT) rules and finally capital allowances (CA) – further explained in Chapter 5.

Accountancy and audit fees – IT: allowable. Strictly, fees for tax compliance work by accountants is not allowable, but this point is normally ignored. Costs of tax appeals and tax planning advice are not allowable. VAT: input tax is deductible.

Advertising and publicity – IT: normally allowable. This is true even if you also intend someone else incidentally to benefit (as with ads in the church magazine or at the local football club). Permanent signs are capital – you may get a CA.

Bad debts – see **Debts**

Bank charges – IT: allowable on business accounts. See also **Interest**.

Books and magazines – (Can you get the tax back on this book?) In practice, books and journals bought for the business may be allowed, although strictly magazines are a revenue expense and allowable, whilst books are capital, and eligible for a CA. This rule will apply if you buy a major work. There is no VAT on books or newspapers.

Business gifts – see **Entertainment**

Capital expenses – IT: not allowed as deductions, but CAs can be claimed. See Chapter 5. See also **Renewals**. Proper capital expenses can be allowed for CGT. VAT: there is no distinction between capital and revenue expenses, so the input tax can be claimed unless disallowed expressly.

Charity payments – IT: will be allowed if you make reasonable payments to charities in the interests of your business, but disallowed if for the benefit of the giver's family or not for the business. Both individuals and companies can separately claim tax relief for a **Covenant** to a charity. Companies (but not other traders) can deduct up to 3% of their dividends for the year as allowable expenditure on a charity. All employers can operate a deduction system for their employees, so the employees give up to £240 a year to charity free of tax. Businesses can also second staff to a charity and still claim a deduction for their pay. For advice on any of these points contact the Charities Aid Foundation at 14 Bloomsbury Square, London WC1A 2LP.

Clothing for work – IT: 'smart' clothing for work is not allowable, even if you *only* wear it at work. If you need a uniform (evening suit for a musician or waiter) or special protective clothing (boiler suit, safety wear), this is allowable. VAT: protective clothing is not VATable where the wearer buys it.

Compensation and damages – IT: payment of compensation or damages to a customer or after an accident from the business accounts is not usually deductible – unless the injury or damage occurred as part of the process of earning the business profits. The moral is to insure properly, as general **insurance premiums** are deductible if they relate to the business.

Covenants – IT: the cost of a deed of covenant to a charity is deductible against the total income of an individual or company, but not against the *business* profits. Covenants must be in the correct form and last four years or more in normal cases. Covenants have been used widely to cut tax on payments to students and after a divorce, and in some other cases. Most of these uses were stopped in 1988. See also **Charities**.

Debts – IT: in most cases accounts are based on money earned by the business even if not yet received. Debts are not allowable as deductions except when they become *bad debts*. This means they remain unpaid after all reasonable attempts to collect have been made, or where the debtor is insolvent. A bad debt allowance is not allowable. When a bad debt is later paid, the debt must be added to the business income. Debt collecting costs are allowable. VAT: roughly the same rule applies, except that relief by reclaim of the output tax is restricted to cases where debtors are insolvent. Both tax and VAT problems can be avoided if your accounts are on a **cash basis** rather than an **earnings basis**. See Chapters 3 and 10 about this.

Depreciation – IT: although all well-drawn accounts should allow for depreciation of the value of capital items, this is never allowable in tax accounts, or for CGT purposes. Instead, the profit may be reduced by any CAs allowable for plant and machinery, or other limited kinds of expense. See **Capital expenses** and Chapter 5.

Directors' fees – if the business is a company, directors' fees are allowable for corporation tax purposes, but there are special rules for tax and NI preventing the use of loans to directors avoiding this tax charge.

Dividends – if the business is a company, its profits are paid out to shareholders as dividends (unless already spent, eg, on interest or directors' fees). Dividends are not allowable against profits for corporation tax purposes. When a company makes a dividend payment, it must also pay ACT to the Revenue (see Chapter 6).

Entertainment and business gifts – IT: most forms of business entertainment and gift are expressly disallowed as deductions against business (or employees') income. The only exceptions are costs of entertaining staff of the business, and small business gifts. But these must:

- cost £10 or less, incorporate a conspicuous ad for the business, and not be food, drink or tobacco; or
- be free gifts to the public generally made for advertising purposes; or
- be items normally supplied by the business in its trade (eg free samples).

VAT: input tax is not allowed for business entertainment. Supplies of business gifts will normally be supplies in the course of business, and therefore taxable outputs on which VAT is payable. See also **Charity payments**.

Equipment – major pieces of equipment (such as a designer's drawing board or computer hardware) will be capital expenses and CAs will be available. Expendable equipment, or equipment with a short life, will be treated as allowable revenue expense – for example, pens, knives, machine ribbons, brushes, cups and saucers. See **Renewals**. VAT: input tax on all these items is deductible.

Fines and penalties – IT: fines, penalties and related legal expenses are not deductible where incurred by the business owner, on the grounds that they cannot be incurred for the purposes of the business if it is run properly. Payment by an employer of staff fines, such as a parking fine for a van driver, may be allowed.

Franchise fees – IT: this is not straightforward, because it depends what the franchise fees are for. Initial payments *may* be capital and not allowable, but if they are payments for services, eg training, they will be. The annual payments will partly be for services and use of copyright, and allowable.

Gifts – IT: gifts to employees are deductible if genuine work expenses but not if excessive. Free samples also allowable, but for limits on other business gifts see **Entertainment**. VAT: gifts are supplies and therefore VATable.

Health costs – IT: medical bills, health insurance and other costs incurred on yourself are not allowable, even if they are incurred in order to save your business lost profits. Health costs of employees are, however, deductible. VAT is not payable.

Heating, lighting, power – IT: allowable if incurred for the business. If the cost is for heating part of your home used for the business, a reasonable apportionment should be allowed. VAT is not payable.

Hire purchase, credit sale – IT: the cash price of the goods, leaving out all VAT, is capital on which a CA can be claimed. A deduction can also be claimed for the **Interest** in most cases. The VAT can be claimed as input tax.

Improvements to buildings and equipment – IT: improvements are capital and therefore not allowable (compare **Repairs**), although CAs may be allowable for improvements to equipment.

Income tax and other taxes – IT: not surprisingly, you cannot deduct the cost of one tax bill against profits to reduce another tax bill, so income tax, CGT and corporation tax are not deductible, although **rates** and **NI contributions** are (but only for half of your own Class 4 contributions). If you are a registered trader, leave all VAT out of your income tax accounts, both input tax and output tax. If you are not registered for VAT, it should be included with the expenses.

Insurance premiums – IT: premiums incurred for business purposes, eg insuring premises or staff, are deductible (and see **Compensation**). No VAT is payable.

Interest – IT: interest incurred by the business for business purposes (eg a general bank overdraft) is deductible, as is the cost of interest incurred by a partner borrowing money to buy into a partnership or buying equipment for the partnership. Other incidental costs of loans, such as commissions, are also deductible. There is no VAT on interest.

Land and buildings – IT: the cost of buying land and buildings, or erecting a building is capital, and is not allowable. CAs are available for industrial buildings and agricultural buildings, but not for shops, offices, warehouses or private houses (with limited exceptions). See also **Rent**.

Leasing costs – these are normally deductible. See Chapter 5.

Legal expenses – IT: allowable if spent on getting legal advice about something which is itself a revenue expense, eg collection of debts or entering a lease. Legal costs on capital items (eg setting up the business) and on non-business expenditure, eg where the owner is defending a drink-driving charge, are not allowable. Lawyer's fees are subject to VAT, which is deductible if the fees are.

Life assurance – IT: premiums for polices taken out on the life of a key employee (eg top salesman) are deductible if the policy is short term (five years or less). Premiums for other policies are not deductible. VAT: no impact.

Loans – (see also **Interest**). The cost of a loan made by, but not repaid to, the business is only deductible if it is the practice of the business to make loans. The same is true where someone is required to pay out on a guarantee of someone else's loan. The repayment of a loan or mortgage by the business is a capital payment and not deductible in the accounts, although it may be relevant to CGT. Incidental costs of loans, eg brokers fees, are allowable.

Losses – see end of this chapter.

Motor vehicles and their running costs – the capital cost of a vehicle gives rise to a claim for a CA, although there are limits on the amount of CAs claimable for cars. The cost of leasing a car is deductible, as are the running costs such as petrol, repairs and servicing, insurance, licence (though employees may be taxable if you supply them with a car and free petrol or servicing). The sale of a car is exempt from CGT, though tax may be payable if other vehicles are sold at a profit.

VAT is payable by the business if it supplies its cars at a charge, if it sells cars at a profit, or if it supplies petrol for private motoring. As an anti-avoidance measure, if a sole trader supplies himself with petrol for private use, he must pay a scale charge, but can then claim the VAT on all petrol bought whether for business or private use. The scale figures vary from year to year, and on the size of the car, but are around £20 a month. If you spend less than about £50 a month on petrol, it will be cheaper not to claim the input tax on petrol at all, and avoid the scale charge. But check the right figures for your car and business.

NI contributions – IT: the cost of the employer's Class 1 contribution for any employee is deductible in full. Half the cost of Class 4 contributions of the self-employed are deductible, but Class 2 and Class 3 contributions cannot be deducted.

Pensions and pension contributions – IT: pensions payable to former staff and their families are allowable. It is normal to buy pensions through approved pension funds. Contributions to approved funds, both for yourself and for your staff are fully allowable. Further, the income of pension funds is tax free. You, and your staff, only get taxed when the pensions are paid.

Personal expenditure – IT: this is never deductible. VAT: input tax cannot be reclaimed on personal expenditure, although if something is bought partly for the business and partly for private use, an apportionment can be agreed.

Political contributions – IT: not deductible, unless (exceptionally) it can be shown that the cost is incurred for the purposes of the business.

Postage, delivery charges, stationery – IT: allowable in full. VAT is not payable on postage costs, but is payable on delivery services.

Pre-trading expenses – see **Setting up the business**

Rates – IT: allowable on the business premises (but not on private premises where the rate is lower).

Renewals – IT: costs of renewals of small items of equipment, or replacements of parts of capital equipment are allowable, even though the original purchase was capital.

Rent – IT: allowable, although see **Land and buildings**. VAT is not payable on rent.

Repairs and improvements – IT: repairs to buildings and other assets are allowable expenses for income and corporation tax, although improvements to those assets are not allowable (except insofar as they make repairs unnecessary). Improvements which increase the value of the asset at the time of sale are deductible instead for CGT purposes. VAT is payable on repairs and alterations.

Research and development – IT: allowable under special provisions, even though speculative, and whether revenue or capital, provided it is incurred for trading purposes.

Royalties – IT: payments of patent and copyright royalties are deductible. They are liable to VAT, so input tax is deductible.

Setting up the business – IT: the initial costs of the business, eg, legal fees, costs of setting up a company, interest on loans taken out before the business starts, travel costs and so forth are claimable under special provisions set out in Chapter 7. VAT: input tax can only be claimed from the time the business becomes registered for VAT, or such previous date as you and Customs may agree.

Social security – see **NI contributions and Pensions**

Staff costs – IT: allowable in full, including all cash pay, provision of benefits in kind, pension contributions, NI employer's contributions, staff welfare costs, entertainment of staff (only), but not if the level of pay (eg to members of the family) **is excessive for the work done**. VAT: paying staff is not a supply, but making gifts in kind to them may be.

Subscriptions – IT: payments to trade associations and professional bodies are normally allowable. VAT is not usually payable on such payments.

Technical education – IT: the costs of a trader paying for a college to provide technical (but not general) education for employees is allowable – even if the employees are his own children. So is the cost of sending employees for re-training.

Telephone – IT: allowable if for business use. If the phone is used both for business and privately, the call charges and rental should be split. VAT: is payable on telephone bills.

Theft, and other crime – IT: the cost of stock losses and cash losses caused by criminal actions of staff and customers are allowable, but losses where, eg, a director or partner commits a major fraud on the business are not (though insurance premiums for insuring against such losses are allowable). Loss of a capital asset through theft amounts to a disposal for CGT causing an allowable loss (unless the asset is insured, in which case it is treated as being sold for the insurance money. If the asset is replaced from the insurance money there is no charge). Damage to assets is treated as a part-disposal for CGT purposes (see Chapter 5), but money spent on repairing damage is allowable for income tax, and not deductible for CGT purposes.

Trading stock – IT: cost of purchase allowable in full. The cost (or value if lower) goes in each year's accounts (see Chapter 3). VAT payable on buying trading stock is fully recoverable against VAT on selling it.

Travel costs – IT: costs incurred exclusively for the business are allowable in full, including incidental hotel, etc, bills, as is the cost of travel abroad on business to see customers or to attend conferences. Taking your wife or husband with you is not allowable, unless it can be shown that this is also solely for business purposes.

Use of home as office – see Chapter 11.

Tax treatment of losses

Where someone makes a loss rather than a profit, there will be no tax, because this is treated as being a profit of nothing. Fairness requires that the loss be set off against other profits, to stop the taxpayer being overtaxed in total, but this does not always happen. Different rules apply to different kinds of losses and different taxes.

Trading losses

If a taxpayer makes a loss from a trade or profession, **loss relief** is available. The loss can be set off against any other taxable income in the year in which the loss is made. Because most businesses run on the **preceding year basis** of accounts, that means the loss can be set off against the *previous* year's profits. It can also be set off against any other kind of taxable income that year of the taxpayer, or the taxpayer's husband or wife. If that does not provide enough of a cushion, it can be carried forward one year and set off against any income of the following year. The example shows how.

EXAMPLE

Claiming tax back on trading losses

Sarah runs a small shop, which is usually quite profitable, but in the trading year 1986 she made a £1,000 loss. The accounts of her business are run on a calendar year basis. Sarah's husband, Tony, is a well-paid company executive.

Sarah's tax loss is treated as being made in the tax year 1986–87. In that year she would normally be taxed on the profits made from her shop in the calendar year 1985. So, for tax purposes, she can deduct the £1,000 loss against the 1985 profits before paying tax.

If the 1985 profits were under £1,000, she would pay no tax on them, and could set off any unrelieved loss from 1986 against any other income she has. If she has no other income, it can be set off against Tony's salary.

In 1987–88, Sarah would normally be taxed on the 1986 trading profits. She will therefore pay no tax on her business that year.

Where this rule is not enough to allow full relief, (or where, for example, Sarah does not want her losses set off against her husband's income), the unallowed loss can be carried forward to set off against the next taxable profits of the business. Special rules apply to losses in the first years of a business (see Chapter 7), in the final years of a business (see Chapter 12), and when a business is turned into a company (see Chapter 6).

The effect of these rules taken together is that a taxpayer (or a husband and wife, or partnership, or a company) can set tax losses from one trade against either profits on another trade, or against any other kind of earned or investment income. This provides some sort of cushion both against the lean periods of a business, and against starting in a risky business.

Losses on income from land

Losses on income from land (because revenue outgoings exceed the rent) cannot be set off generally against income. They can be set off against any past or future rent from that property under that lease or tenancy. Relief against other rented properties is only allowed under limited conditions if the landlord is running them properly for profit.

Other losses for income tax purposes

The general rule for other kinds of losses (eg Schedule D Case VI) is that they can only be set off against other income that year, or in the future, of the same kind either of the taxpayer or the taxpayer's husband or wife. The system assumes that losses do not occur on investment income.

Capital losses

The rules for CGT (and capital losses, made by companies) are the same as the 'other' losses from income tax. Losses are worked out in the same way as gains (see Chapter 5). Any losses are set first against gains that year, with any excess losses being carried forward against future gains. Losses cannot be set off against trading or other income for income tax purposes, except for the special reliefs mentioned in Chapter 7.

Losses and VAT

If you have a VAT loss, you will have paid out more VAT on inputs than you have collected on outputs. This happens regularly in zero-rated trades. In any such case, you can claim the excess VAT back from the VAT Office.

Is it a deductible expense for income tax?

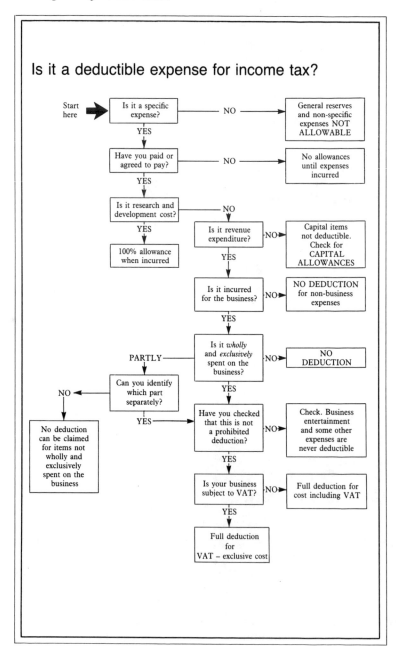

5 Is it an asset?

Income tax deals clumsily with business and personal assets. Perhaps we should feel sorry for the poor old thing – after all, it was invented during the Napoleonic wars, before anyone had thought of railways, companies, or electric lighting, and when the Foreign Office had just 13 full-time staff! In those days, business assets consisted of millwheels, waterwheels and slaves on the sugar plantations. Small wonder the rules don't really work on computers, satellites and milk quotas.

Though the world has changed just a little since then, the basics of income tax have not – so rules dealing with capital assets have had to be added on. This is done by two sets of provisions:

- income tax allowances for the cost of capital purchases are provided for only in the form of **capital allowances**, and
- profits from sales of capital items are taxed by the **capital gains tax** not income tax.

This chapter examines both.

Capital allowances

Income tax works on the basis that costs of new capital items, such as machines or new business premises, do not count against profits in the same way as revenue expenditure. Capital expenses are long-term, so are only allowed against profits a part at a time. Most accountants agree with this, and deal with capital expenditure by a **depreciation** provision in the accounts. The Revenue do not accept depreciation as stated in the accounts as a deduction for tax purposes for two reasons: because the law allows deductions only for some kinds of capital expense; and because it sets a standard rate of deduction (while each accountant is free to choose individual rates of deduction for individual clients).

What expenses can be claimed

Capital allowances are available only for the following types of expense:

- *Plant and machinery* – this is very wide and covers all sorts of equipment. In practice it is relevant to all kinds of business.

- *Industrial buildings* – such as a factory, but not a building used mainly for an office, shop, warehouse, or home, so this is chiefly important only to the manufacturing trades.

- *Specialised allowances* – allowances are available to some special industries: for agricultural land and buildings, mines and quarries, dredging and the oil industry.

- *Research costs* – research and development expenditure is allowable in full, whether the cost is revenue or capital.

Apart from these allowances, no deductions are available. For example, a retail business can claim allowances on the shop equipment (such as freezers or cash tills) but not the shop building.

Does it matter how I buy?

A business can acquire the use of business assets in four main ways:

- *Outright purchase* – either from its own resources or on an overdraft or loan facility. If a capital allowance is available, it can be claimed when the asset is acquired. Any interest is deductible from trading profits.

- **Leasing** – this does not involve buying the item at all. Consequently, no capital allowance can be claimed. Instead, the full cost of leasing rentals is allowable against profits if the asset is used exclusively for the business. The leasing company will usually be claiming a capital allowance for its purchase of the item, so the lessee can benefit from the tax relief indirectly in the leasing rates charged. If there is a final capital payment, or balloon payment, at the end, that may not be allowable.

- **Hire purchase** – credit sale or other instalment purchase schemes. Here the buyer pays the seller or finance company for the item and for interest on borrowing the outstanding amount, plus any fixed charges. The buyer is treated for capital allowance purposes as buying the item outright at the date of the agreement, and then paying the interest and charges separately. Any capital allowance can be claimed from the date of the agreement, even though the asset is not bought until later. The buyer then claims a deduction against profits for the interest when paid, deducting any fixed charges in the first year.

- **Contract hire** – don't buy or lease the equipment at all. Instead, contract out the work for which the assets are needed to a sub-contractor. It will be the sub-contractor's job to buy or hire the equipment (or use assets already partly in use for something else). You pay the total bill which is fully deductible for income tax, regardless of the capital costs involved.

Planning purchases wisely

You can see that these are genuine choices. Which should you choose, and what other points should you watch? There are two key differences between contract hire and the other alternatives. First, the full cost of contract hire and leasing is deductible against tax. Assuming you make a profit, and pay tax, that makes the real cost of contract hire or leasing significantly cheaper than the cash rental. It is still not cheap because there is a hidden finance cost in it, so get comparative figures before deciding this way. Second, contract hire does not appear on the balance sheet of the business, because you do not own anything. This is often referred to as **off-balance sheet finance**. It reduces the assets of your business, which is sometimes an advantage, sometimes not.

Buying from your own resources often looks the cheapest option but it is only superficially so. Work out what else you could be doing with the money. If it could earn more elsewhere, you lose those earnings whilst buying the equipment. Take a simple example. I intend to buy a car with my savings. It will cost £8,000. At the moment the savings are on long term deposit earning 8% interest before tax. If I buy the car, I will be losing income of £640 a year before tax (rather less when the tax is knocked off). If I keep the car for one year, it may well lose, say, £2,000 in value. I have therefore lost not only £640 *this* year, but at least £160 *every* year on the depreciation of the car. Could I have done better – should I buy a cheaper car?

Time it right

Plan when it is best to buy. You get the same capital allowances granted at the same time on your purchase whether you buy at the start of the accounting year or at the end. The later in the accounting period you buy, the quicker you get some of your money back. That's not advice to delay – it's advice to think ahead, with perhaps an eye to buying at the end of the previous year. Particularly if you're buying on hire purchase, or with any sort of interest holiday (that is, free credit period before you start paying interest), an agreement signed just before the end of a year has an advantage over one signed just a little later.

Watch the VAT as well. You will be entitled to get the **input tax** on your purchases back, but only by setting them against your **output tax** at the end of each return period. It is therefore best to pay a bill with a significant amount of VAT as near the end of the return period as possible. But again, if the equipment is going to earn you money, it is not worth waiting for that reason alone – rather it may be better to bring the **tax point** forward to an earlier account period, even if the cost is still met later.

'Plant and machinery'

These words are taken from the tax laws, but they get no proper definition there. They cover all forms of equipment (rather than buildings or the setting of the work) bought for any kind of business, including all the following:

- advertising and publicity screens
- air conditioning, space heating and similar equipment
- alarms and security devices, including fire safety expenditure to meet Fire Brigade requirements and other safety equipment
- books, manuals, guides (but journals are revenue expenses)
- canteen or other amenity expense, eg cooking equipment and crockery (though replacements will be revenue expenses)
- carpets and other detachable floor covers, curtains, blinds
- cars, vans, lorries – even horses – if used for the business
- costs of removing or demolishing old machines
- equipment of artists and craftsmen, such as looms, potter's wheels, kilns, drawing boards, musical instruments, even disco equipment
- fees incurred directly in connection with acquiring new plant, eg engineers or architects' fees, but not fees related to financing the equipment
- installation costs of machinery, including costs of altering buildings
- lifts, elevators, cranes and similar equipment for lifting or transporting people or goods
- lighting equipment designed for display or to create an 'atmosphere', eg in a restaurant, but not ordinary light fittings
- machinery for any industrial or commercial purpose
- moveable office or shop partitions, counters and fittings (but not fixed screens or shop fronts which are part of the structure)
- office equipment such as calculators, computers and their peripherals, typewriters, storage cabinets, dictation equipment, photocopiers
- office furniture, eg chairs, tables, cupboards
- paintings, sculptures, murals, tapestries, prints, etc where these are purchased to create 'atmosphere' as in a hotel
- telephone equipment, faxes, telex machines.

Allowances for equipment

'Plant and machinery' does not cover buildings or anything forming part of them (such as light fittings, central heating, water supplies) or their grounds (such as car parking spaces). Allowances are fully available only if the items are used solely for business purposes, and are of a kind justified by the business. If a newsagent decides, on winning the pools, to deliver his newspapers by Rolls Royce, the Tax Inspector is unlikely to be convinced that this choice of car is justified by the business. An estate agent who gives customers a lift to properties in an expensive Porsche can argue that he needs a good car to impress them.

How the allowance operates

A business which spends sums on plant and machinery in any year can deduct part of the cost in that year and future years until the full cost is met. The amount allowed each year is usually 25% of the cost of the item so far as this has not been allowed in previous years. The following example explains how this works.

EXAMPLE

Buying equipment: the capital allowance

Cath buys a piece of equipment worth £1,000, and claims the 25% allowance on it.

Year 1:
She spent £1,000 and claims 25%, so she deducts £250 against her income tax profits. This reduces her tax bill by £62.50 if she pays at 25%, and £100 if she pays at 40%.

Year 2:
She has had no allowances on £750 (£1,000 less £250). She claims 25% of this £750, a total of £187.50.

Year 3:
The amount left over from last year is -562.50 (£750 less £187.50). She claims 25% of this, amounting to £140.62

[and so on . . .]

The table in the next box is a 'ready-reckoner' on the allowances year by year on an initial cost of £1,000.

The rules assume that assets normally last at least five years. In cases where this is not so, the business can get allowances over the life of the item, if the owner notifies the tax authorities that he is claiming for a **short life asset**. The cost is then spread over the likely life of the item.

Annual capital allowances on equipment costing £1,000

year 1 : £250
year 2 : £187.50
year 3 : £140.63
year 4 : £105.47
year 5 : £ 79.10
year 6 : £ 59.33
year 7 : £ 44.50
year 8 : £ 33.37
year 9 : £ 25.03
year 10 : £ 18.77

In practice, equipment will often be replaced before it has worn out, and before the annual capital allowances is negligible. In addition, businesses will have a number of assets on which they are claiming allowances. How does this work?

Selling or scrapping assets

If a piece of equipment is taken out of use by the business, the owner may have claimed either too much capital allowance (because the asset is sold for a profit) or too little (because they scrapped the item, but have not had all the price allowed). To deal with this, the allowances are adjusted by a series of **balancing charges** and **balancing allowances**.

Balancing charges

A balancing charge operates when an item is sold for more than the amount of capital allowance unclaimed at the time of sale. If, say, Cath sold the equipment she bought for £1,000 in year 2 for the sum of £800, what would the position be? She has claimed allowances of £437.50 (£250 and £187.50), so has £562.50 unclaimed. But she is getting £800, so there will be a balancing charge on her of £237.50 (£800 less £562.50).

The balancing charge is added to the profits of the business for the year, and thereby increases the profits so the Revenue recover the tax.

Balancing allowances

A balancing allowance works the other way. If Cath scrapped her equipment in year 2 because new technology made it worthless, and she only received £50 scrap value for it, she made a loss. She had only £437.50 in allowance, but has spent £950 in total on the machine after recouping the scrap sale proceeds. So she is entitled to a balancing allowance of £512.50 (£950 less £437.50). This balancing allowance is a deduction against profits, so will reduce Cath's tax bill noticeably.

Pooling

When a business has more than one item of plant and machinery on which it is claiming capital allowances (as is usual), the different allowances are **pooled**, to use the jargon. This means all allowances and new claims are added together each year, then adjusted for all balancing allowances and charges, and the final amount is available for that year's allowance. The example shows how this works, assuming Cath buys a new item costing £1,000 each year, and scraps the first item for £50 scrap value as just discussed.

EXAMPLE

Cath's pooled allowances

Year 1:
Item 1 bought for £1,000. Allowance £250 (see above)

Year 2:
Item 2 bought for £1,000. 'Pool' is £750 for item 1 and £1,000 for item 2, total £1,750. Allowance £437.50

Year 3:
Pool from previous year: £1,312.50 (£1,750 less £437.50). Add cost of item 3: £1,000. Add balancing allowance on item 1 (scrapped for £50): £512.50. Total pool now £2,825.50. Allowance £706.25.

Allowances on cars

Restrictions operate on allowances for cars costing over £8,000. You cannot claim the 25% allowance on more than £8,000 in any year. The total unallowed cost is carried forward and kept subject to this ceiling until the unallowed cost for a year is below £8,000. To let this happen, the cost of cars caught by this rule must be left out of the 'pooling' of allowances. You cannot sidestep this rule by leasing a car, because the same limit applies there. If you lease a higher-priced car, only a proportion of your leasing costs are allowable against tax (the proportion £8,000 bears to the total cost).

CGT and equipment

Special rules apply to the charge of capital gains tax (or corporation tax on chargeable gains of companies) on equipment on which a capital allowance is granted. These rules are designed to prevent a double allowance or charge to both income tax and CGT. When an item on which a capital allowance has been granted is sold, CGT is only charged if the sale proceeds exceed the original cost of the item. It is limited to the excess. This rarely arises, but when it does a charge to CGT can be avoided if the sale proceeds are reinvested in replacement equipment. In most cases sale proceeds will be less than the original cost. That loss is not allowable for CGT purposes.

Buildings and workshops

A highly advantageous special allowance operates alongside a rather ungenerous main rule. First, the full cost of a wide range of buildings in **Enterprise Zones** can be set off against income tax straight away, or as much of the cost as the taxpayer wants to claim. This is a most generous allowance for capital cost and explains why so much new building takes place in these zones.

The general rule is that expenditure on buildings and land does not qualify for any allowances at all. This is because buying land and most kinds of building is an investment which will pay a handsome profit in any event, and in the meantime will save the owner significant rent costs. Some kinds of industrial building do get a limited relief.

Industrial buildings

You can claim limited relief on any building if you incur capital expenditure on buying or constructing a building or structure which is used only for a trade involved in manufacturing, processing or stockholding goods, or for a trade carried on in a mill or factory or similar buildings, plus mining, agriculture and some other special trades. To qualify, at least 75% of the building must be used for that purpose. Buildings used as offices, private houses, shops, warehouses, garages or any other purpose not covered do not qualify unless they form part of an industrial building but less than a quarter of it.

In addition to industrial buildings, capital allowances are also available for hotels and for private houses let on assured tenancies – though there are some tight requirements for that kind of allowance to be claimed.

The allowance is a deduction against profits for tax purposes of 4% of the original capital cost each year for 25 years. If the building is sold, let on a long lease, or taken out of industrial use during that time there will be a balancing charge or allowance like that for plant and machinery.

Capital Gains Tax

The key idea of CGT is very simple indeed:

If you have	**A** ssets
which you	**C** hange
so you	**G** ain
you pay	**T** ax

In other words, if whenever you dispose of any capital item, you show a profit, you are liable to CGT on the gain, unless you are entitled to some relief.

What items are covered?

CGT taxes all kinds of property unless the particular item is exempted. It potentially covers anything you can sell or make money out of – even rights to sue someone, rights to share in someone else's profits or an employment contract. Business assets which will be caught include:

- land and buildings, and any interest in land, such as a lease or advertising rights
- investments such as shares, debentures, some forms of government stock (National Savings and some government stocks are exempted)
- machinery and equipment worth over £3,000 and sold at more than the purchase price
- rights under contracts, and to take legal actions against others
- valuable objects such as paintings, antique furniture, valuable books, unless held by the owner as stock in trade (eg for an antiques business)
- goodwill on a business.

Assets not taxed

The main exemptions are:

- **Your only or main home** – but only if you use it all as a home. If you use any part of it exclusively for your business, or for letting, you risk losing part of the exemption.

- **Cars** – but not vans.
- **Objects worth less than £3,000** – when you dispose of them. But if, say, you try and break up a set to cut the value of the parts below £3,000, that won't work. It's the full set that counts. This rule does not apply to land, or to investments such as shares.
- **Things with an expected life of under 50 years** – when you get them, other than items used in a trade. This removes most household items.
- **Money** – in sterling, but not profits or losses made on foreign currencies.
- **Debts** – that is, the right to receive money at some future time; but this does not cover secured debts such as mortgages, debentures and government stock.
- **Life assurance policies** – held by the original owner.
- **Insurance policies** – where the item insured is not itself a chargeable item (eg personal injuries insurance). Where the insurance is of, say, a building which is chargeable, and a claim is made, the building is, in effect, treated as sold for the insurance proceeds, with the loss on the building being cancelled out by the gain under the policy.
- **Trading stock** – this is because trading stock gets fully taxed by income tax.

Disposal

There is a liability to tax, or a right to claim a tax deduction, whenever a taxable asset is disposed of to make a gain or a loss. 'Disposal' means any kind of transfer from a person of her or his rights to it, for example, sales, leases, mortgages, exchanges, gifts or the loss or destruction of an item. There is a disposal whenever part of an asset is disposed of or a capital sum is derived in some way from an asset. For example, part sales of land include selling off part of the land, selling a lease over the land, or selling someone the right to park cars on part of it or to extract minerals from it. What it really comes to is that if you have a taxable item, and you make a capital sum out of it, CGT will apply unless one of the exceptions operates.

Important exceptions to tax include charities and gifts to charities; pension funds; employee trusts; heritage property, and trusts and bodies looking after the national heritage (such as famous works of art and stately homes, universities and libraries).

Gifts not taxable

Transfers between husband and wife do not attract tax. More generally if the giver of a gift and its receiver agree, they can jointly notify the Tax Inspector that they want to postpone the CGT that would otherwise be payable when the gift was made.

Under the normal rules, a gift (or a sale at a deliberately low value made non-commercially) is treated as a sale at the market value of the item given. CGT is payable if that produces a gain. If the giver and receiver choose, they can treat the receiver as getting the gift at the price paid by the giver. For example, if Zale gives Faw shares worth £10,000 in the family business which Zale originally obtained for £500, Zale will be liable to tax. If Zale and Faw agree, Zale is treated as selling the shares to Faw for £500. If Faw sells the shares, tax will be payable on the whole gain since Zale received them.

Rollover-relief on business assets

A potentially damaging charge to CGT could arise if a business sold one of its assets with the intention of replacing it. For example, Zale sells a shop in Borchester with the intention of buying one in Ambridge. Under the usual rules, CGT is payable on the sale of the shop, leaving less money to plough back into the business. A 'rollover relief' exists to prevent this happening. If you sell a business asset, but use the proceeds within a period starting 12 months before the sale and ending three years after the sale to buy a replacement asset of the same kind, then any gain made on the sale is 'rolled over' on to the new asset. This is done by reducing the cost of buying the new item for CGT purposes from the price you paid for the new asset by the amount of the gain made on the old asset. When you finally sell up, tax will be payable on both sales.

Relief for those over 60

Because of rollover reliefs on business assets, and gifts on which tax is postponed, much of the CGT payable during the life of a business can be postponed. But until when? Usually the rollover stops when the owner sells up and retires. This leaves a potentially heavy charge hanging over the business when someone gets older, just when they want to take money out to sort out their retirement. To avoid this charge being too heavy, a special relief operates, as explained in Chapter 12.

Working out gains and losses

If the sale proceeds exceed the deductible expenses, there is a **chargeable gain**. On the other hand – and just as important – if the expenses exceed the proceeds, there is an **allowable loss**. Losses are calculated in exactly the same way as gains. Loss relief is described in Chapter 4.

The sale proceeds are treated as being the amount actually received if the disposal was a commercial one. In other cases, as with gifts or sales between relatives, the market value of the items at the time of disposal are treated as being received as sale proceeds. This applies where the asset was bought or acquired since 6 April 1982.

Only new gains taxable

CGT is only chargeable on gains made since 6 April 1982 (or 1 April in the case of companies). Where an asset was owned on 5 April 1982 some of the gain made on a disposal will relate to the time the asset was held before that date. If the item has been held for a long time, much of the gain might therefore be outside the taxable period. How is this handled? The main rule is that the item is treated as being bought on 5 April (or 31 March) at its market value on that date. This will require the expert guessing of a valuer in some cases. The value at that date is treated as the purchase price, and the gain worked out against it.

Allowable expenses

This is dealt with partly in Chapter 4. The CGT rules are that expenses of the following kinds are the only ones deductible:

- purchase costs, or costs of making the item (or the price on 5 April/31 March 1982 if the asset was owned then)
- incidental costs of purchase (legal fees, surveyors fees)
- costs of enhancing the value of the asset, reflected in the value at sale (but not running repairs)
- costs of protecting ownership of the asset, (eg legal costs of fighting a claim by someone else to ownership)
- incidental costs of sale, (eg estate agents fees, advertising costs).

Keep records of all capital expenditure, and of the purchase price of capital items whether acquired before or after March 1982, together with details of all costs of selling the assets. This will make accurate claims for allowable expenses much easier. If a cost is deductible for income tax, it is not also deductible for CGT.

Indexation allowance

One trouble with CGT is that it taxes cash gains, rather than real gains. That is, it taxes the almost inevitable rise in values caused by inflation along with the actual gains in real terms. To avoid that, an **indexation allowance** is added to each item of expense. It is the amount by which the cost of living has gone up since the expense was incurred (or on the value at March 1982 if later) up to the month in which the sale took place. The Revenue regularly publish tables of these allowances. They are reprinted in most tax journals and are available in most good libraries.

The rates of CGT

CGT is charged on the total taxable gains in any income tax year, that is, the net amount of gains less losses for the year. The first £5,000 (in 1988–89) is free of CGT (the figure varies from year to year); the rest gets charged at the appropriate rate of income tax: 25%, then 40% or at the corporation tax rate for a company.

How CGT works

EXAMPLE

Let's tie all that together with an example. Our old friend Zale bought a shop as a going concern back in 1973, and sold it in June 1988 also as a going concern. The price was £80,000 for the freehold of the shop, fittings, goodwill and stock at valuation. Zale paid £10,000 in 1973, and it is estimated that the market value was £60,000 in 1982.

For CGT purposes we ignore the stock, as that is included in the income tax calculations. We must also break up the sale price to isolate any sums paid for exempt assets, and also for equipment on which capital allowances have been paid (as these are ignored for CGT purposes unless they are sold at over cost). Let's say we remove £5,000 from the price for these. The rest is for the building, fixed assets and goodwill.

Zale's price was £80,000, but there will have been lawyers' fees, estate agents' fees, stamp duty and other selling costs. Let's say they totalled £4,000. Zale bought the shop in 1973, so for these rules, we need the market value at March 1982. The total value was £60,000 then, so ignoring equipment, etc, it would have been about £56,000. Zale has had no capital expenditure on the shop since 1982 (that's to keep it simple – in reality there would probably have been some allowable expenditure on improvements).

What gain did Zale make? To find that out, we must first find out the indexation allowance from March 1982 to June 1988. In the tables it is (we'll say) 0.300. Zale's allowable expenses are increased by that amount, that is, the £56,000 value of the shop in 1982 is increased by 0.3, bringing it up to £72,800. The sale proceeds less expenses came to £76,000. The chargeable gain is therefore £76,000 less £72,800 or £3,200. Zale will pay tax on that at 40% (say), a total tax bill of £1,280. If Zale buys another shop to replace the one sold, that tax can be postponed until the new shop is sold.

6 Taxpayers Co Ltd?

It may be, as it says in '*The Importance of being Earnest*' that in married life three's company and two none. In business, two, or even one, can be a company, but that does not make it a good idea. Before you rush off to set up your business as the United Metropolitan Improved Hot Muffin and Crumpet Baking and Punctual Delivery Company (Limited by Shares), or whatever, a word of warning. It may actually cost you more in tax than if you leave your business unincorporated – or it may not. Particularly since the 1988 tax reforms, this needs careful thought. That's what this chapter is about.

Whether or not it is an advantage for tax reasons to be a company rather than a partnership or a sole trader is just part of the story. The limited liability or apparent status of a company may be of sufficient value to offset the extra costs. I looked at these points in a special chapter in *Running your own business*, and shall not cover the same ground here. That chapter also looks at **partnerships**, when two or more individuals (or companies) are carrying on business in common with a view of profit. Again, we will not repeat here what is said there, but look at taxation of partnerships at the end of this chapter.

Why companies are important

The key legal point about running a business through a company is that it is legally separate from you. Let's say you are running your own small business, and you want to set up a company to run it for you. You will, presumably, sell your business to the company, but you will go on handling the business on behalf of the company, of which you will be managing director. After that, you are no longer self-employed. The company is boss, and you are its employee. Further, the company will not pay income tax and capital gains tax. Instead, it is required to pay **corporation tax** on both its income profits and its gains, whilst you will pay tax (and NI contributions) *as an employee* on your earnings.

The corporation tax

As we have seen, British companies cannot pay income tax or CGT, but must pay corporation tax. There are some important differences between CT (as we call it for short) and income tax and CGT – particularly the rates. The current rates are set out in the box attached. The highest rate of CT is 37½%, less than the top rate of income tax or CGT. Whilst the rate on a small company is the same as the lower rate of income tax (25% at present). The times of payment and some other details are different. However the key rules, about how big the profits of the business are, and what expenses can be deducted, are almost the same for companies as for individuals. Where they differ, they tend to be slightly more generous to companies.

Rates of corporation tax: 1988

Main rate of tax 35%
(Paid by companies with profits over £500,000.)
Small companies rate 25%
(The small companies rate is payable by companies
with total profits under £100,000.)
Rate on profits between £100,000 and £500,000 .... 37½%
(**25%** is payable on profits below £100,000)

What kind of company?

For tax purposes, there are two basic sorts of companies: **trading companies**, which carry on some selling or servicing business, and **investment companies**, or holding companies, which are used as 'vehicles' to hold property or shares in other companies. In practice, companies frequently operate in **groups**, with one or more holding companies holding all the shares in separate trading companies. There are special rules for handling the taxation of groups of companies, but they are beyond the scope of this book.

Of course, a trading company may have investments and investment income, and a holding company may in part be involved in a trade, but the two kinds of income are best kept apart. In particular, there are special anti-avoidance tax rules aimed at small companies with investment income. The problem is that a company can be used just to save tax on investments. The company will pay tax on the income at the CT rate. It will not pay income out to its owners, so they can avoid the higher rate of income tax. This does not, however, apply to trading income, with which we are chiefly concerned in this book. On the other hand, an investment company is allowed to deduct its expenses of management when calculating its tax, where an individual cannot.

Anyone wishing to handle investments on any scale through a company should keep this separate from his or her business, and obtain separate advice about it.

Taxing a trading company

The profits of a trading company are calculated for CT purposes in just the same way as profits of an individual are calculated for income tax, except:

- **Interest payments** – companies can deduct all interest payments against profits before calculating the amount of tax. (They are known as 'charges on income'.) This replaces the individual's mortgage relief.
- **Charity payments** – the company can deduct payments under covenants as charges on income, and also a total of 3% of the income distributed as dividends.
- **Capital gains** – gains on sales and so forth are worked out in the same way as for CGT, but the amount is added to the total of taxable profits when working out how much CT is payable.
- **Dividends** – companies pay profits to their shareholders as dividends or distributions. When they do so they must pay **ACT** (advance corporation tax) as explained below. They cannot deduct the cost of dividends against profits.
- **Payment** – this is always to be paid, at the latest, nine months after the end of the accounts year.

A company running a business must be registered for VAT separately from its owners, if the level of turnover of the company is over the levels requiring registration (see Chapter 10).

Paying money out of companies

Profits earned by a company are the property of the company, not of its owners or employees, and the company pays tax on these profits. Note how those profits may then be paid over to the owners or employees. In the case of the smallest companies, there are usually just a few people who own the company by owning all the shares. The owners will often also be the directors of the business and its employees. They may also provide working capital to the business by way of loans. And they can wind the company up if they so choose. How the profits are paid to them will reflect these ways of controlling the company.

There are four ways the money can be paid out. First, as **earnings** to the directors or employees – either in cash or by benefits in kind. Either way, the company can deduct the cost of the pay and benefits in working out its taxable profits, so long as the payments are made for work actually done. The company will operate the **PAYE** scheme and pay the earnings with tax deducted.

Secondly, the money can be paid out as **interest** on loans made to the company. This will be appropriate if the owners choose to limit the amount of money they put in by buying shares, and provide extra capital in the form of loans. Again, interest is deductible against profits for tax purposes. When the company pays out the interest, it must deduct basic rate tax and account to the tax authorities for it.

Next, the money can be paid out as **dividends** on the shares. When this happens, the company has to account for **ACT** to the tax authorities. As we see below, this is the equivalent of deducting basic rate tax.

Finally, the money can be paid out as a **cash payment** to shareholders on **winding up** the company. This used to be a way of reducing tax – but since 1988 things have changed and it may now increase the tax instead. How? Because the payment is a capital gain to the shareholder and that now bears tax at the same rate as income tax.

Apart from a liquidation (when the company is lost), basic rate tax is therefore deducted, so does it matter how payment is made? As between interest and dividends, the importance is that money tied up in shares is less flexible than money tied up in loans. It can be arranged that the interest paid on the loans is related to profits, making it much like a dividend. It is far easier to alter loan arrangements than to alter share capital. The owner will pay the same tax either way.

If the owner is paid earnings, more tax will be payable. This is because the earner, and the company, must both pay NI contributions on earnings. Even on higher earnings the company must still pay standard rate NI contributions (currently at 10.45%). Of course, the earner will be entitled to a pension in due course, but if the earner has already paid maximum NICs, this will gain nothing extra.

ACT and taxes on dividends

When a company pays a dividend to shareholders, it must also pay ACT (advance corporation tax) to the Revenue. The rate of ACT is currently $1/3$. This means that if the company pays out, say, £75 as a dividend it must pay $1/3$ of this, £25, to the tax authorities. To pay out a dividend of £75 the company must therefore have £100 available. Looked at the other way, the dividend is paid to the shareholder at £75 plus a tax certificate for £25. The shareholder is treated as receiving a total payment of £100, with the basic tax of £25 paid. This system must be operated whenever a company pays out money, except on a liquidation or when it is paying back share capital.

To make this work, the company must provide the shareholder with a **certificate of deduction**, along the lines of the one in the following box:

Wibble Widgets Ltd: Dividend and tax credit

I hereby certify that Wibble Widgets Ltd paid to William Wibble the dividend stated below on 31 March 19★★ in respect of ordinary shares for the year ending on 31 March 19★★.

Amount of dividend £.......... Tax credit £ ....

I further certify that advance corporation tax of an amount equal to the sum shown above as the tax credit will be accounted for to the Collector of Taxes.

31 March 19★★   Zale Fothering
                                                    Company secretary

---

Unlike interest or earnings, dividends cannot be deducted
from profits for tax purposes by a company. Instead, the
company can treat the ACT as an advance payment of its CT
bill, both on income profits and capital gains. As the rate of
tax on a small company is also 25%, the effect of this is to
cancel out the tax liability in full. Although the method is
different, the end result is much the same to the company as
a deduction. This will not be so for larger companies.

Tax on sales of shares

The ACT system is designed to avoid double taxation of
company profits. This would happen if the company paid
tax on the profits, and then the shareholder would pay it all
over again when the profits are paid out at dividends.

Double taxation does occur on capital gains of companies. If
a company makes a gain, it pays tax at its CT rate. The rest
of the gain goes to increase the company's assets, and therefore
the value of its shares. If the shareholder sells the shares, or
the company is wound up, he or she will pay tax (at 25 or
40%) on the gain made in selling the shares, including the
gains already taxed. The effect is double tax. For example, a
small company pays tax at 25%. Its shareholders pay tax at
40%, £100 gain to the company will leave £75 in assets.
Assuming that is reflected in the company's shares, and all
the shares are then sold, the £75 share value will get taxed at
40%, or £30. This leaves only £45 of the £100 in the
shareholders' hands.

To make matters worse, a **stamp duty** is payable on all sales
of shares. The duty is ½% of the total value of the shares,
though it can be avoided if the shares are transferred by a gift
or on death.

This double taxation is a problem in transferring businesses
from a company to individuals, or winding up the company.

Once a business has been transferred to a company, it can be expensive to get it back out.

Transferring a business to a company

There is a risk of a charge to gains tax when a business is transferred by individuals to a company, because they are treated as disposing of the business to the company at its market value. That causes a substantial CGT bill on the individuals in many cases. It can be avoided only if the whole business (excluding only cash) is transferred to the company, and the price paid by the company is issuing its shares to the individuals.

Not all tax can be avoided in this way. One problem is that the roll-over relief from CGT on replacing business property (see Chapter 5) will come to an end, forcing tax to be paid on bills that were earlier postponed. There is also a risk where a loss-making business is transferred to a company that the transfer will cause the benefit of the tax relief on losses to be forfeited. The loss relief can be carried forward under a special provision, but only if the transfer is wholly or mainly in exchange for shares in the business, when the income from those shares will be treated as trading income against which the loss relief can be set.

Company or not?

Although as a general rule it is, for tax reasons, much less worthwhile putting a small business in a company in 1988 than it was in 1979, there is no one answer as to whether it is better for tax reasons to run a small business through a company. Check the following:

Checklist: Tax on companies and individuals

- *Tax rate on profits*: CT rate on small businesses is 25% up to £100,000, while individuals pay 40% over about £20,000. Trading income can be held by the company, so the 40% rate does not have to be paid, but investment income must be taxed as though the shareholders had received it, as most trading income if paid out.
- *Tax rate on gains*: same tax rates as income, *but* tax gets paid by both company and individual on gains, making the total rate over 50% in many cases. The double charge does not arise until shares are sold, or the company is wound up, but is a marked disadvantage of trading via a company.
- *Time of payment*: companies pay tax at ACT on paying out dividends, and in any event nine months after the tax year. Individuals can pay much later than that (see Chapter 13).
- *Stamp duty*: payable at ½% on sales of shares, but not usually on business assets (other than land). None on partnership assets.
- *Earnings of owners*: if owners receive money as earnings, NI contributions are payable as well as PAYE tax, which noticeably increases its cost. Earnings are available for use in paying tax-free pension contributions, but so are earnings of self-employed. However, companies can generally contribute more to provide pensions for their employees than the self-employed can contribute to their own personal pension.
- *Special reliefs*: reliefs on retirement or death, or for gifts of shares in a family company and of a business are much the same. However, it is easier to transfer parts of a business in the form of shares, so companies can ease problems of estate planning for inheritance tax.
- *The costs of changing*: changing a business into, and especially out of, a company can itself be expensive for tax reasons.

A note on partnerships

Partnerships do not exist, but yet cause some of the worst business tax problems there are. How come? In England and Wales (but not for the wiser Scots) the law says that partnerships do not have any separate identity – there are only the partners. Income tax is therefore payable by partners

as individuals on trading or professional profits of the
partnership. Each partner is fully liable for all the tax due
from the partnership in that year.

What causes the real problems is the **preceding year rule**.
This year's partners get taxed on last year's profits. But what
happens if the partners have changed, or if the partners' profit
shares have changed – or if one partner is paying tax at 40%
whilst the others are paying at 25%. The Revenue's answer
is simple – it doesn't really care as long as someone pays it
the tax due. That leaves the partners arguing about who pays
what share of the tax bill. That's not easy. If you are likely
to run into that problem, get expert advice.

7 Grants and incentives

To see the full picture of our tax system we must look at both sides of the canvas – not just what the Government gets out of your business, but what your business can get out of the Government. These are two parts of one system. It doesn't always look that way in the UK, because the money coming back sometimes appears as tax reliefs and sometimes as grants, with different government ministries involved. Here we bring these provisions together to allow an overview. In doing so, we are concerned only with provisions of central and local government, and the European Communities, not with private grants, even those provided by charities or otherwise indirectly assisted by taxpayers.

Special tax reliefs

Aside from general tax reliefs available as part of taxing any business, such as interest and loss reliefs and capital allowances, there are a number of special reliefs designed to encourage the setting up of new businesses. First, there are reliefs against income tax to assist new trades and those investing in them. These are:

- initial loss relief
- pre-trading loss relief
- venture capital loss relief
- the business expansion scheme.

Then there are two special kinds of area where businesses get tax advantages over other areas. These are:

- enterprise zones
- freeports.

Special provisions also operate in Northern Ireland.

Initial loss relief

When a new business is started, it often has losses in the first few months because of heavy initial expenditure being incurred before the income starts flowing. Under normal rules this can be set off against any other income of the business owner in the year in which the loss is incurred or in later years (see Chapter 4).

There is a special relief allowing the business owner to recover tax paid in years before the business began. This applies where someone, for example, gives up a salaried job to become self-employed. The relief can be claimed where a loss is made by an individual in the first year in which a trade is carried on, or in any of the next three years. If it is claimed, the loss can be carried back three years and set off against income of that earlier year. The relief must be claimed against an earlier year rather than a later year.

EXAMPLE

The relief works like this. Say that a business is started in June 1986. Relief is available for any losses in the tax years from 1986–87 to 1990–91. Say that a loss is made in the first year, 1986–87. This can be set off against income in the years back to 1983–84, starting with that year, then going to 1984–85 and 1985–86. If the relief is claimed, it will operate by reducing the income for 1983–84 first. If, say, this results in a reduction of £5,000 in the income for 1983–84, the taxpayer will then be able to claim back the tax paid on the top £5,000 of his income that year. This will result in a repayment of at least 30% (that year's basic rate and perhaps 60% (that year's top rate). This means a relief for the loss of anything from £1,500 to £3,000.

Pre-trading expenditure

Linked in practice with that relief is another allowing pre-trading expenditure to be regarded as spent when the business first starts. The general rule is that expenditure is only allowable during the course of the business. On that basis, anything spent before the business starts would be disallowed. However, a special relief allows a deduction against trading profits of expenditure incurred not more than three years before a business starts but for the purposes of the business. The cost is treated as incurred on the first day of business, and is therefore relevant for initial loss relief.

There is also a VAT problem with such expenditure. If expenditure is incurred before the business is registered for VAT, the business will be unable to recover the VAT paid on the inputs. Further, the business will not have to register until its turnover on outputs reaches the threshold figure (see Chapter 10). To avoid high levels of VAT being paid out before it can be recouped it may pay a business to register voluntarily. This it can do since 1988 once it intends to carry on a business, or has started doing so, regardless of turnover.

Venture capital loss relief

Individuals who invest in unquoted shares in a UK trading company can claim an additional relief if the shares are disposed of at a loss. The relief applies only if the loss is realised because of a commercial sale of the shares, or because the company has gone into liquidation or the shares are of negligible value. When that happens, the shareholder can choose to have the loss treated as a loss for income purposes instead of the capital loss it would normally be. Whilst the top rates of income tax and CGT are now the same. This may still be an advantage in allowing the relief to be set off against income, for example, when there are no taxable gains against which to claim the relief (see Chapter 4). It therefore amounts to a small additional incentive to invest in unquoted shares.

The Business Expansion Scheme

Individuals who subscribe for new ordinary shares of an unquoted UK trading company as an investment can, if they meet the conditions of the business expansion scheme, claim a deduction against income tax for the amount invested. Relief is not available if the individual is an employee or paid director of the company, or is associated with it in a number of other ways. Nor is it available for shares other than those issued new to the subscribers. The intention is to encourage outsiders to invest in new businesses carried on by others.

For a company's shares to be approved for BES deductions, it must be carrying on one or more trades of a kind approved by the rules and meet other limits laid down (for example, it cannot have more than half its assets tied up in land, or be a dealer in commodities, shares or stock). The individual must invest at least £500 in the new shares, and is expected to maintain the investment for several years. If he or she gives the shares away during the period of five years from the start of the business, the tax relief is lost. Similarly, if he or she sells the shares during that period, the tax relief is reduced by the amount received back on the shares (effectively taxing the full price received).

Individuals are entitled to deduct up to £40,000 a year against their taxable income in connection with investments in BES companies' shares. Assuming the investor is paying tax at the higher rate, this means that he or she gets tax relief of £200 for each £500 invested in the year of investment. This explains the attractiveness of the scheme to higher rate taxpayers.

However, the scheme involves quite complicated legislation, so any business seeking to attract investors who would claim BES relief on their investments will require proper advice from accountants or solicitors with appropriate experience.

Enterprise zones

Enterprise zones (EZs) have been set up in areas of industrial dereliction, and inner cities, all over the country (the Small Firms Service will give you details). There are two significant tax advantages to any business operating in an EZ:

- Full (100%) capital allowances for income tax and CT purposes on the cost of new or rebuilt industrial premises, offices and commercial properties and hotels;
- No business rates.

Both these reliefs – and several other non-tax reliefs – operate for a period of ten years from the time the EZ was started. They operate in addition to any regional grant aid that is available.

Freeports

Half a dozen freeports have been set up at air- and sea- ports in the UK. Each is a secure area where goods are free of customs duties and VAT until they leave the freeport. This allows goods to be imported and stored until wanted for sale without the cash-flow disadvantage of having already paid the VAT and duty on them.

Northern Ireland

In an attempt to encourage further investment in Northern Ireland, it has special tax privileges compared with Great Britain. For example, all industrial premises are exempt from rates. A number of generous Government grant schemes are available, part of which are free of tax. Further grants are available to refund corporation tax to companies in respect of up to 80% of the tax on profits from approved projects. To find out about these as they operate for small firms (those employing under 50 people), contact the Local Enterprise Development Unit in Belfast.

Grants and loans

Separate from these special tax reliefs, considerable assistance is available from public bodies out of money raised on general taxes and rates. These are part of a variety of separate schemes from different Government departments, many local authorities and from the European Communities. Some are in the form of grants, others as loans, grants to pay the interest on loans raised privately, or provision of guarantees either of risks being undertaken by the business or of loans taken out by it. Some operate only in certain localities, others only to certain industries. Some are well-known, like the help to farmers, others get much less publicity. Yet all are provided by public funds to encourage businesses – and especially small businesses – to get started and to expand.

What grants and loans are available?

It would take a book quite a bit longer than this one to answer that question in enough detail to cover all the options available at a national level, because the answer varies so much from one area to another, and from one kind of business to another. Keeping tabs on all these forms of help, and on the changes to them from time to time, is now so complicated that more than one major bank has installed a full computer–based service to check out what is available for customers. Some accounting firms have done the same thing.

Because of this wealth of detail – all of which is important to some businesses – it would be misleading to pretend we could give you full details here. What we shall do is to tell you of the main sorts of help available, and then where to check whether there is any help for you.

Regional assistance

The map on page 92 shows areas of Great Britain designated by the Department of Trade and Industry (DTI), the Scottish Office and the Welsh Office as:

- Development Areas ⎫ together known
- Intermediate Areas ⎭ as Assisted Areas
- Urban Programme Areas

Any business in an Assisted Area can apply for **regional selective assistance**, by way of grants, to help it undertake a business project in the Area. The amount of grant awarded to any one project will be a matter of negotiation between the DTI (or Scottish or Welsh Offices) and the grant applicant. Grants are awarded as a matter of discretion of the government department. To qualify for one, the applicant will have to show that the project is financially viable, that it will produce some regional or national benefit, and that it will either create or safeguard employment in an Assisted Area.

Small firms (those with under 25 employees) in Development Areas, can benefit under a further scheme which provides investment grants to help buy new fixed assets and to help approved innovations – for innovations up to half a cost of £50,000 will be met.

In Urban Programme Areas, generous finance is available for projects designed to help create employment or to benefit the area. Although Government-funded, these schemes are run in partnership with the local authorities of each inner urban area. To find out more, contact the local authority for the area, which should have appointed an Industrial Liaison Officer to deal with the schemes.

Other regional aid is separately available from other bodies as well. In England, the Development Commission (incorporating CoSIRA, the Council for Small Industries in Rural Areas) gives aid for small businesses, such as craft businesses setting up in **Rural Development Areas** – defined separately from the Assisted Areas. In Scotland, special help is available from the Highlands and Islands Board, and in Wales from Mid Wales Development – again, separately from assisted area status. These areas are shown on the map on page 93.

Sector support

What? Taking out the jargon, this means help available to particular kinds of business. There are a wide variety of different kinds of help to be considered, depending on what kind of business is involved. At the one extreme, there are businesses which have for years enjoyed generous support in the form of grants. Two such industries are farming and bus transport. Both are getting shaken up these days by the withdrawal of the grants on which whole businesses have long depended for their financial viability.

The change in the bus industry outside London was immediate and dramatic when it was deregulated a few years ago. There is chaotic overprovision in some places (as anyone living near Oxford knows), whilst there are no services at all in other places, even though subsidies may be available. Farming is another business in a process of quite sharp change. Prices are dropping, and quotas are cutting production whilst costs of production go on rising. It is said that over 20% of all our farmland must go out of production in the next 20 years, and the grants scheme will reflect this.

One rural answer will be tourism, and the English, Scottish and Welsh Tourist Boards run Government–funded schemes of grants and loans to help develop tourist facilities. It is but one answer. Check what others may be available to help you.

Help with employment and training

The biggest Government schemes of the lot are those run by the MSC (Manpower Services Commission) to help train both the young and those going into new businesses. Best known is the **YTS** – the Youth Training Scheme – aimed at providing training and work experience to any unemployed young person between 16 and 18 years of age. If your business can provide the work for someone under the YTS scheme, then you will, in effect, get the assistance of that young person at greatly reduced cost. This is because the government pays a YTS trainee direct for her or his work. Many small businesses have benefited in this way, whilst providing valuable opportunities for the young to train. Could you?

MSC also provide other financial aid to local colleges and other bodies to provide training and retraining courses and programmes. These are always worth checking on, especially as there are now a wide range of courses available to the small business owner.

Assisted Areas after November 28, 1984

Rural Development Areas, Steel Closure Areas, Highland & Islands
Development Board and Mid Wales Development

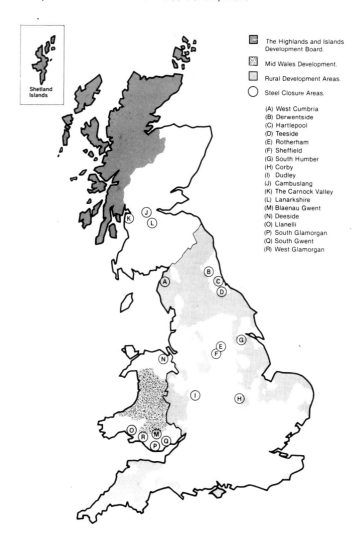

The Highlands and Islands
Development Board.

Mid Wales Development.

Rural Development Areas.

Steel Closure Areas.

(A) West Cumbria
(B) Derwentside
(C) Hartlepool
(D) Teeside
(E) Rotherham
(F) Sheffield
(G) South Humber
(H) Corby
(I) Dudley
(J) Cambuslang
(K) The Carnock Valley
(L) Lanarkshire
(M) Blaenau Gwent
(N) Deeside
(O) Llanelli
(P) South Glamorgan
(Q) South Gwent
(R) West Glamorgan

Shetland
Islands

Enterprise allowance

This £40 a week starting payment to anyone previously unemployed is noted fully in Chapter 9. It is paid by Jobcentres. Enterprise Allowance is taxable, and someone claiming it may be liable to Class 2 and Class 4 NI contributions.

Tax and grants

The general rule is that money received as a grant is to be taxable on if under income for income and corporation tax purposes. It must therefore be entered into the profit and loss account in the same way as ordinary trading income. This does not apply to grants specifically for capital investment. These will be taken into account, instead, in calculating capital allowances and any chargeable gains if the new assets are sold. There are some kinds of grant which are in effect tax free but these are increasingly uncommon outside Northern Ireland. These general rules also apply to any other form of grant from a charity or private body.

How to find out more

The two Government departments most concerned with grant support to industry and commerce both run free telephone information services. The DTI runs the **Enterprise Initiative** which provides some of the grants mentioned above, plus other grants designed to make existing businesses more efficient (for example, by paying part of the cost of the time of a consultant to check your marketing or design). Get further details or find out who to contact by ringing **0800 500 200**.

The Department of Employment is responsible for the Small Firms Service. The SFS runs a business information service nationwide, which will give details of any kind of Government grant, or who to contact to find out the details. Again, it runs a free telephone service. Ask the operator for **FREEFONE ENTERPRISE** and you'll be put in touch.

You will also find your local library ready to assist. Main libraries in most parts of the country now run specialist information services for businesses, and again will put you in touch with local contacts. Another contact in a number of areas is through the local authority's Industrial Liaison Office or Economic Development Office (the names vary but the job is the same), which has the task of encouraging local initiatives.

Many private bodies will also help, but two in particular must be mentioned: the local enterprise agencies (there is a nationwide network of these business advice bureaux) and the Prince's Youth Business Trust (which was established by the Prince of Wales specifically to help those aged from 18 to 25 years). Full details of these bodies are set out in *Running your own business*.

8 A tax on your staff

If you run your business through a company your 'staff' will include you. In any other case, you should have some staff, even if only your wife or husband paid to help you part-time, and to take advantage of available tax allowances. This chapter examines how staff are taxed, whether managing director or part-timer, to see the difference tax rules may make in the way people are paid.

What taxes apply?

Two – income tax as it applies to earnings (**Schedule E**), and NICs paid by employees and directors (**Class 1**).

Who are the 'staff'?

That sounds a daft question – don't you know who you employ? Well, maybe not, and with good reason, for there's a knotty legal problem we need to look at. It's the answer to the question: what's the difference between being employed and being self-employed?

One way out of problems about staff is not to have any. OK, you need work doing, but you get it all done on a sub-contract basis. There are sound management and cost reasons for using self-employed sub-contract labour, even leaving tax totally out of account. For tax reasons, sub-contract labour is often easier and may look cheaper, so some people try and get all their 'staff' treated as sub-contractors. It does not always work.

Employed or self-employed?

The difference is stated by lawyers as the distinction between a **contract of service** and a **contract for services**. Whether a particular contract is '*of* service' or '*for* services' depends on all the facts and circumstances, and not just the bits a written document includes. The key issue is the relationship between the individual and business involved. There must be some form of agreement if there is to be a contract of service. How the DSS look at this is set out in the following box.

A works for B: Is A employed by B?

The DSS look at the following pointers as indicating A is employed by B:

- A is required to give personal service to B, for which A is paid.
- A is part and parcel of B's business.
- A is subject to B's control or right of control as to what is done and when and how it is done.
- B has the right to select, suspend or dismiss A.

The following indicate A is not employed by B:

- A is not required to do the job personally.
- A is paid by the job, rather than on an hourly or weekly basis.
- A is in business independently, with B having little or no right to dictate hours or methods of work.
- B is not concerned whether or not A is making a profit.

Problem areas

The vagueness of the test makes it inevitable that there are areas of dispute. The DHSS (as it was) and Inland Revenue have both been pushing for some time to get the groups of people who are regarded as employees expanded, and to cut down on those who are regarded as self-employed, especially in areas of abuse (such as television staff, musicians and teachers) and where a lot of part-timers work. Their reasons are obvious – to get PAYE working, and to get higher contributions. By contrast, VAT officers look for the self-employed, because employees cannot be registered persons in respect of their employments.

Who decides?

Just to confuse things further, each of the taxfolk make their own minds up about the status of a taxpayer. It can therefore happen that the Revenue regard someone as self-employed, while the VAT people regard the same person as employed. The DSS make it worse by having rules (called **Categorisation Regulations**) which decide the status of some borderline cases – but they don't apply to the Revenue or VAT Office. Recently (at last) the Revenue and DHSS (as it was) have got their act together and will accept each other's guidance. Ask either for an official ruling if in doubt.

DSS categorisation rules

- A husband can employ his wife as an employee to help him with his work, but she cannot be self-employed for this purpose. If he employs her for any other reason (such as to do 'his' housework) this is totally ignored. (The rule also works the other way round if the wife is the employer.)
- Agency workers and 'temps' are regarded as being employed by their agencies.
- Office and commercial cleaners are regarded as being employed by whoever pays them, whether this is the business where the cleaner works or an agency.

Income tax on employees

The rules charging income tax on employees (and directors) (known as Schedule E) catch the full amount of earnings from all employments, less only limited expenses. No problem normally arises with payments in cash. In practice, a wide number of fringe benefits are commonly paid, to save tax. These are caught in different ways, as noted below.

NICs on employees

These work under different rules to Schedule E. Liability on an employee's (or director's) earnings is to **Class 1 contributions**, payable by both employees and employers. There is little problem with cash payments. There are no NICs on benefits in kind or provision of accommodation or meals. Consequently, once it is decided whether a person is or is not an employee, there are few disputes about contribution liability.

18 ways to pay your staff

The tax (IT) and contribution (NIC) rules on particular benefits are:

Accommodation – IT: detailed rules about this charge tax on the employee, unless the employee is required to live 'on the job', eg caretaker or warden. No NICs on board and lodging.

Bonuses – if paid in cash are treated the same way as ordinary earnings both for IT and NICs. There may be advantages in paying these near the end of a tax year to reduce company profits, or to use up tax allowances or the 25% tax band. See also **Profit related pay**.

Cars – employer can deduct full cost (NB limits on capital allowances); employee taxed on tariff figure on both car and free petrol (charge is about half true value to employee). No NICs on employee or employer. Special VAT rules apply. The car tariff figures were increased sharply in 1988 – check cars are still worth giving. If the employee uses a car for less than 2,500 miles of business motoring, the tariffs are increased sharply. That's why visits to distant customers seem so necessary every March.

Cheap loans – cost (if any) to employer allowable. Employee earning over £8,500 charged on benefit (ie difference between interest charged and market rate) if the benefit exceeds £200. No NICs. No VAT.

Expense accounts – employer costs allowable. Employee earning over £8,500 taxed on full amount of account, unless can claim deductions. No NICs.

Gifts – IT: employer cost allowable *if* gifts of reasonable amount and genuinely for business purposes (which includes improving staff morale with, eg, wedding presents). Employee not taxed if genuine gift, and not disguised pay (eg annual Christmas bonus). No NICs. VAT may apply.

Meals, luncheon vouchers – IT: employer costs deductible in full. Benefit to employee of free meals in canteen tax free. First 15p of Luncheon Vouchers tax free, rest taxable. No NICs. Is VATable.

Paying employee's bills – employer cost deductible, but fully taxable on all employees, and NIC liability on full cost to employer. Not usually worth doing.

Paying employee's tax – bar exceptional cases, don't – it just increases the costs. Employer's cost deductible, but employee treated as earning the amount paid by the employer, thereby increasing the tax bill further (and if that met, extra tax again and so on). NICs will be leviable on this amount as cash payment.

Pensions – IT: the best bargain of the lot. Employer's annual premiums fully allowable; employee's annual premiums also fully allowable; employee not charged on employer's contributions. NICs: no deduction for pension costs, but no charge on employer's contribution. No VAT.

Professional advice – if you provide your staff with free professional services, eg health monitoring, or financial counselling and advice, there is no tax or NICs for them to pay. You pay the VAT of course.

Profit related pay – it's complicated, but if you set up a profit-related pay scheme, so that employees get up to 10% of their pay on a profit related basis, half the profit related pay is tax free. That's the up side – the down side is: no profits, no pay.

Removal expenses – IT: allowable if reasonable costs and move is required by employer (or new employer) – also some help with other relocation expenses and cost of new house. NIC: not levied on these payments (perhaps because the Revenue are one of the most generous payers of relocation costs!).

Staff discounts – IT: employer can deduct cost usually just part of general stock costs). Employee not taxable unless employer provides goods at below cost. NICs: not charged. VAT will apply if goods are VATable.

Staff entertainment – IT: cost allowable if genuine staff entertainment. No charge on employees. NICs: no charge. VAT may be payable.

Travel costs – IT: employer's costs deductible. Charge on employee depends on how it's done, eg, if employer reimburses employee's costs – charged in full; employer cheap loan to buy season ticket – charge on interest if employee earns over £8,500; employer supplies employee with ticket – employee taxed on cost to employer; employer provides own transport – no cost to employee. NICs: no charge if no cash. No VAT.

Uniforms – no IT or NIC charge to employee.

Work expenses – if you refund genuine work expenses to an employee or director (eg for travel at work, but not to/from work) it is not pay, so no IT or NICs on the employee.

Higher paid staff

The list shows some benefits taxed only on staff and directors earning £8,500 a year or more. These staff (called **higher paid employees** in the rules) have their benefits in kind dealt with under a stricter code designed to catch all expense accounts payments, plus other benefits such as cheap loans and the loan of equipment (such as videos) for private use. To allow the Revenue to monitor the rules, employers must submit special returns (on Form P11D) to the Revenue for higher-paid members of staff and directors, indicating benefits received. In working out the £8,500, account has to be taken of all benefits. The rules apply to company directors with any level of earnings, unless full-time working directors with only a small share in the business.

Company directors and NI

There are no special rules for higher paid employees for NICs purposes, but there are for company directors. These are designed to prevent you playing around with the way directors are paid (for example by means of loans rather than earnings) to avoid NICs. Full details are set out in DHSS leaflet NI 39, *Company Directors and NI*.

One practical point – see Chapter 6 – is that directors of small companies are usually also shareholders and can be paid either earnings or dividends. Payments of dividend saves no income tax, but it does save NICs, and is therefore worth considering in some cases.

The best way to pay

There are savings for both employer and employee in the way the staff are paid. Check the following example for an idea.

EXAMPLE

How much is the new dress?

Sue and Kate both want new dresses costing £50. Kate has to buy hers, while Sue can get hers from her employer, as she works in a dress shop. Kate buys hers at full cost out of taxed income. At 1988–89 rates, she is probably paying income tax at 25% and NICs at 9%. To earn the £50 net to spend on the dress, she must earn £76.

Sue earns a bit less than Kate, but gets other benefits. She can buy clothing at cost from her employer. This has a hidden VAT saving in it as well as the direct saving on the retail margin. Sue's employer sells her the dress she wants for £25 (costing her £38 in earnings). She gets the same dress as Kate, but earns £38 less to get it. Does her employer lose out? Not as much as at first sight. If he pays Sue a bit less than Kate, he will be saving the employer's NIC on her pay (at 9% or 10%). He can still claim the cost of the dress in full against his profits for tax, and some VAT may be saved. And it may actually increase his sales!

Sue's employer could go a stage further, by insisting that Sue wore certain of his products whilst at work, and supplying them to her free on loan. Unless she is higher-paid, she pays no tax on a loan. The employer will of course want his staff to look good in a dress shop to maximise business. If the employer does that, Sue pays nothing for the dress. She may be very happy to wear such good clothes, particularly if she is £76 better off than Kate. There is also no NIC supplying a dress for Sue's use.

What of VAT? If the dress is used only for work purposes, there is no VAT to pay, because there is no supply. If it is used sometimes by Sue for private use, the employer should account for VAT, according to the rules, by dividing the cost of supplying the dress to her, after allowing for what it is still worth, between its use at work and its private use. That will probably not be much.

This is a simple example, but shows how the reinforcing of income tax, NICs and VAT mean that a bit of sensible planning allows employers to provide more value to employees at lower cost.

Paying your wife

In many cases where a husband is self-employed, his wife is not working. He can therefore pay her for helping him, so as to use up the wife's earned income relief, and the band of pay on which no NI contributions are payable – currently about £40 a week. This can be further supplemented by tax-free benefits. For example, if the husband pays contributions to a non-contributory personal pension for the wife, this will be a deductible cost for the husband's business, but will not be taxable to the wife (or incur NI contributions), subject to premium limits. Had the wife not been paid anything, the pension contributions would not be permissible as deductions. The key issue is whether the cost to the husband's business is justified by the work the wife puts in, she must be doing something to earn her pay.

Rates of tax

The rates of income tax are 25% and 40% in 1988–89.

There are several rates of NICs. There is a minimum weekly earnings figure below which no contribution is payable, either by employee or employer. In 1988–89 this is **£40.99**. Above that figure, earnings are liable to contributions under **Class 1** of the NI contribution structure – a **primary** contribution payable by the employee, and a **secondary** contribution payable by the employer.

Depending on both the overall weekly earnings of the employee, and his or her status, a set percentage of all earnings (including those below the minimum) is collected from both the employee and employer. See the rates box. One look at it will show that there are certain important thresholds in levying the tax, when the cost to both employer and employee of small rises in pay is quite large. For example, work out the contributions payable when an employee earns £105 a week, compared with £104.

NIC Class 1 rates 1988–89

The percentages apply to the whole pay of the employee, unless otherwise indicated.

Weekly amount	employee contracted-in	employer	employee contracted-out	employer
0 – 40.99*	0	0	0	0
41 – 64.99	5	5	3	1.2
65 – 104.99	7	7	5	3.2
105 – 154.99	9	9	7	5.2
155 – 304.99	9	10.45	7	6.65
305 plus (on excess over 305)	0	10.45	0	10.45

* Where employee is contracted-out and earns over £41, the contracted-in rates are payable on the first £41.

Special low rates apply to certain married women and widows entitled to pay at a reduced rate (but not their employers). Those over retirement age (65 men, 60 women) pay no contribution, but their employers pay the normal rates.

Pensions and the contracted-out NICs

Pensions are a major point to consider, whether paying yourself as director, paying your wife as explained above, or paying any other staff. You do not have to pay a pension contribution (apart from the compulsory NI contributions) either for yourself or anyone else, but there are significant tax advantages in doing so, and it is only sensible to take this into account in your own long-term financial planning at least – even more so as you near retirement.

Since 1988, there has been a new scheme of **personal pensions** in operation. This allows individuals to set up their own pension scheme and claim full tax relief on it (that is, the full contribution can be deducted from income for tax purposes, and the income to the pension fund whilst the funds are invested is totally free of tax).

Personal pensions come alongside the other two pension schemes widely available. First is the state scheme, often called **SERPS** (State Earnings Related Pension Scheme). This you get on the basis of the NICs paid during your working life. (See Chapter 9 for details). It is paid for by the standard rate Class 1 NICs.

Alternatively, employees can belong to an **Occupational Pensions Scheme** run by an employer. Since April 1988 an employer cannot force an employee to be a member of an occupational scheme. However, if the employee is a member, and the scheme is approved by the Inland Revenue (and there is little point in having one which is not approved), then the member can be **contracted-out** of SERPS, being entitled only to the flat-rate basic retirement pension. If that happens, the employer and employee can both pay a lower **contracted-out rate** of NI contributions, as set out in the box.

The final change is that employees can contract-out of SERPS and have part of their NI contributions directed instead into their own personal pension plan. This could well be an attractive option for younger people as the pension provided in this way could well exceed the benefits provided by SERPS.

What expenses are allowable?

The swift answer is: hardly any, aside from pension contributions. No expenses are allowed at all against NI contribution liability, though this is offset by the rule that benefits in kind and an employer's contribution to a pension fund are not within the NI contribution net.

For income tax purposes, you may deduct subscriptions to certain professional bodies, such as the Law Society (the Revenue have an official list). Travel expenses are allowed only if they are necessary for travelling *at* work. Nothing is allowed for travel *to* work. Other expenses are allowed only if they are *wholly, exclusively and necessarily* incurred in the job. This is a very narrow rule. The Revenue allow certain set (and published figures) of up to about £50 towards special clothing and tools required by employees, but beyond that most kinds of expenses fail the test. The key problem is showing that an expense is necessary – that is, that everyone doing the job must meet that cost.

Collecting the taxes

Nearly all tax on earnings is collected by employers through the **PAYE** system, or Pay As You Earn. This covers both income tax and the NI contributions.

If you are employing anyone with earnings of over £40 a week (or any earnings at all from you, and total earnings from you and others over that total), inform the Inland Revenue and your local Social Security Office (see Chapter 1). They will separately send you full details of how to run the PAYE system.

You will need to keep accurate records for anyone you are paying within the scope of the PAYE deduction scheme, including:

- employee's name
- employee's NI number
- employee's tax code
- dates of all payments
- amounts of all payments (and running totals of amounts through each tax year)
- amounts of any occupational pensions contributions
- amounts of any statutory sick pay or statutory maternity pay
- amounts of any sums given to charity under payroll-giving
- amounts of tax deducted (and running totals of amounts through each tax year)
- amounts of NI contributions deducted
- amounts of employer's NI contributions payable.

This list shows that you must keep full records of all payments to staff and deductions collected from them to comply with the legal requirements of the PAYE system. To help you do this both the Revenue and the DSS provide standard deduction working sheets and forms, supported by explanatory booklets and deduction tables showing how much to deduct in any week or month.

The PAYE system requires all employers to make monthly returns (accompanied by a cheque for tax collected) to the Revenue. This return covers both tax and NICs, and the Revenue pass the NIC cash on to the DSS. A full annual return is also required.

An Inspector at the door

Both the Revenue and the DSS are entitled to send Inspectors
to your offices to check these books without notice and at any
reasonable time. You can be fined for not keeping proper
records, and for not producing them or providing the
authorities with appropriate information if they ask for it.
What is more, they can still collect the tax from you that
you should have collected from your staff – even if you did
not in fact collect it.

More information

Ask your local Tax Inspector or DSS Office if you want
further guidance now. The following guides are available free:
Employers Guide to PAYE (leaflet P7) plus deduction working
sheets and deductions tables; *Thinking of taking someone on?
PAYE for employers* (leaflet IR53); *Tax: Employed or Self-
employed?* (leaflet IR56) – all from tax offices, and *Employers
Guide to NI Contributions* (leaflet NP15); *NI and contract of
service* (leaflet NI 39) (now published jointly with the
Revenue leaflet IR 56); *NI for company directors* (leaflet NI
35) – all from Social Security Offices.

9 When you benefit

This chapter is about two social security systems – the state's and yours,and what you pay and what you get. Many self-employed find the state system inadequate for their needs. That's why they need their own. The tax system can help in giving tax relief if you decide to provide for your own financial security – tax relief not just to you but also to the funds into which your money goes. (If your business is run by a company you are not self-employed – see Chapter 8.)

What you must contribute

The self-employed must make two kinds of NI contribution:

- *Class 2 contributions* – flat-rate weekly contributions payable if you are ordinarily self-employed, regardless of whether you actually do any work in any one week. The contributions are not compulsory for people with low earnings.
- *Class 4 contributions* – an extra levy on income tax payable on trading and professional income (Schedule D Cases I and II, to be technical).

Those not required to pay

Income tax is payable by people regardless of age. Not so
NICs. If you are under 16 or over retirement age (65 men,
60 women), don't pay contributions. Ask your Social Security
Office for a certificate confirming you are not liable to pay,
and send it to your Tax Inspector. You don't have to pay
contributions, even though you have trading income, if you
are not actively engaged in the trade. For example, a **sleeping
partner** in a partnership, who is only investing in a business
run by the partnership, is not self-employed, so does not have
to pay NICs.

NICs for the self-employed: 1988–89 rates

Class 2: £4.05 a week
Contributions are not compulsory for those earning under £2,250 in
the year
Annual maximum of Class 1 and Class 2: £1,455
Class 4: 6.3% of total trading and professional income exceeding
£4,750, up to a limit of £15,860
Annual maximum for Class 4 contributions, with Class 1 and Class
2: £915

Class 2 contributions

These must be paid either by the old-style stamps stuck on a
contribution card, or by direct debit from your bank to the
DSS. Which way you pay is your choice. If you choose to
pay by buying stamps at the local Post Office, get a
contribution card from the local Social Security Office. A
stamp must be stuck on it by Saturday each week.

For details of *Direct debit – the easy way to pay!*, as the DHSS
publicity puts it, get a copy of the leaflet with that title

(leaflet NI 255) from your local Social Security Office. It has Form CF 351 attached, which is what you need to set a direct debit arrangement going. That way you pay about the middle of each month.

Exemption for low earners

If your total earnings from self-employment are likely to be below the threshold figure for the year, you don't have to pay Class 2 NICs, but you may do so if you wish. Why pay when you don't have to? Class 2 contributions give a right to some benefits, particularly basic retirement pension and sickness benefit. If you don't pay, you will have a deficient contribution record, and may lose benefit. So you save now but may lose later. Check your benefit entitlements before deciding which to do. If you do choose not to pay, you need Form CF 10, which you will find attached to DHSS leaflet NI 27A, *People with small earnings from self-employment*, and a copy of which is supplied at the back of the book.

Class 4 contributions

These carry no benefit entitlement. Nor is there any option about paying them. They are collected by the Inland Revenue along with the tax on your trading and professional income. There is a relief available against income tax. You can deduct *half* the cost of your Class 4 contributions against your profits for income tax purposes (though not of course in calculating your profits for Class 4 purposes). This rule does not apply to Class 2 NICs.

People both employed and self-employed

If you are one of the growing number of people who are both an employee and self-employed, you may be required to pay Class 1 NICs as an employee as well as Class 2 and Class 4. If your earnings from both sources are high enough, this may result in you paying too many contributions, as there is an annual ceiling on the total amount of NICs any one individual is expected to pay.

The rules provide that you should not pay more Class 2 NICs than are needed to bring the total of both your Class 1 and your Class 2 NICs up to the maximum Class 1 contribution payable by you that year. They also provide a lower maximum for Class 4 contributions, so that you don't pay Class 4 NICs if you are paying in total under Classes 1, 2 and 4 more than the annual total of Class 2 and Class 4 together.

The annual maximums vary from year to year, and you cannot always tell if you will pay too much. If you think your income may involve you paying too much, apply to the DSS for deferment of your Class 4 (and Class 2) liability. To do this, get form CF 359 which is attached to DHSS leaflet NP 18, *Class 4 NI contributions*, and send it to the DSS Class 4 Group in Newcastle Upon Tyne.

Unpaid contributions

Contributions paid late (that is, after the end of the week or year in which they should be paid) may suffer the penalty of losing the contributor some benefit entitlement, and also having to be paid at the rate set when they are paid rather than when they were due. The DSS have powers to enforce payment or unpaid contributions, partly by prosecuting people for not contributing and partly by civil procedures. Further details, and time limits for using late paid benefits for contribution entitlement, are included in DHSS leaflet NI 48, *NI Unpaid and late paid contributions*.

What you can claim

Class 2 NICs entitle you (or, if you die, your widow) to:

- *Sickness benefit* – payable weekly when you are incapable of work because of some illness or disability. Many self-employed people do not know they are entitled to this. To claim it, you must be off work completely and, if away from work for more than a week, you also need a doctor's sick note. You can use the back of that as a claim form. You cannot, in any event, claim benefit for the first three days of any period of work through illness. If in doubt, contact your Social Security Office. You will also find details in DHSS leaflet FB 28, *Sick or disabled?*. If claiming sickness benefit, you need not pay NICs for any full week of sickness. Instead, you are credited with a contribution. That also applies to the next two benefits.
- *Invalidity benefit* – sickness benefit is available for only six months. After that, the long term sick can claim the long term weekly invalidity benefit for as long as they remain unable to work because of sickness, without paying any further NICs. (For more detail see FB 28, just mentioned.)
- *Maternity allowance* – payable weekly to mothers expecting a baby or just after the baby is born for a period of up to 18 weeks when they are off work. Details are set out in DHSS leaflet FB 8, *Babies and benefits*.
- *Retirement pension* – self-employed contributors get only the basic weekly retirement pension, not the earnings-related supplement. The basic pension can be claimed by anyone over 65 (male) or 60 (female) who has retired from work, but not for those taking early retirement. Full

entitlement to the basic rate pension only goes to those who have paid full Class 2 contributions (don't forget that Class 4 contributions don't count) for roughly nine in every ten years of their full working life. If your contribution record is not this good, you may get a lower weekly pension. Further details are contained in leaflet NP 32, *Your retirement pension*, from the DSS.

The full story for many pensioners receiving basic rate pensions only, even those with a full contribution record, must include entitlement to **income support** (the non-contributory supplementary income benefit) and **housing benefit** (based on the same income levels as income support). This is because the basic rate of retirement pension is below the official poverty level for many claimants. Details of these benefits are beyond the scope of this book. They aim to provide only the minimum level of support.

For details of the retirement benefits, get leaflet FB 6, *Retiring?* from your local Social Security Office. If you are getting near retirement and have a deficient contribution record (for example, because of periods when you were neither employed nor self-employed), you can sometimes pay voluntary contributions known as **Class 3 contributions** (at a little less than the level of Class 2 contributions for each week) to improve your contribution record, and therefore your pension. It's always worth asking.

- *Widow's benefits* – Class 2 NICs also qualify a widow for the £1,000 **widow's payment** when her husband dies, and for **widowed mother's allowance** and **widow's pension** on a weekly basis for widows left looking after children, or over the required age limit for payment. These benefits are payable at the basic rate only, with no earnings related addition. For further details get leaflet FB 29, *Help when someone dies.*

Benefits when starting in self-employment

Many people decide to start their own business because they are unemployed. If that applies to you, you should be receiving either **unemployment benefit** (which is payable weekly for the first year of unemployment) or **income support** (if you have been unemployed for over a year, or if you were not entitled to unemployment benefit because, for example, you had not paid enough NICs). The problem is that you will probably be subject to the 'available for work' rule, and you will certainly be subject to the £2 a day earnings rule. These say that you must be available for work at all times, and you must not be earning £2 a day on any day when you claim to be unemployed.

Because of these, and other rules, people starting in self-employment find they lose benefit whilst not earning anything (or hardly anything) from the new business. If you are in danger of being caught in this position because you intend to start off on your own, apply to your Jobcentre for an **Enterprise Allowance**.

Enterprise Allowance

This is a weekly allowance (currently £40 a week) payable in place of unemployment benefit or income support to people starting on their own. Husbands and wives can both claim separately. Get full details from your local Jobcentre. You must meet the following conditions to be entitled to the benefit:

- you intend to work full-time at a new business, and
- you have not started that business yet, but
- you have been unemployed for at least 13 weeks, and
- you are receiving either unemployment benefit or income support, and
- you are over 17 but under 60 (female) or 65 (male), and
- you can raise £1,000 either from your own resources or as a business loan (eg from a local bank).

If you qualify, see the staff of the Local Enterprise Agency for your area or, if you are under 25, the staff of the local office of the Prince's Youth Business Trust, for advice. They may also be able to help you raise the £1,000. Who they are, and why you should see them, is explained in *Running your own business*. If you do not know where to find them, pick up a phone and ask the operator for **FREEFONE ENTERPRISE**. It will cost you nothing, but the operator will put you through to the nearest office of the Small Firms Service. They will tell you what to do.

Benefits for low earners

If you are just starting in your business, and earning only a small amount – or your business hits a rough patch because, for example, someone is ill – do not forget you may become entitled to **income-related benefits** even though you are still working. These benefits were completely reorganised in April 1988, and there are now three which can help low income self-employed:

- *Income support* – payable to anyone not in full-time employment or self-employment (defined as working for 24 or more hours a week).
- *Family credit* – payable to anyone who is working over 24 hours a week, but has a family (that is, at least one child under 18 living with her or him) and a low income.
- *Housing benefit* – helps people with low or no incomes to pay their rent (either to the local council or to a private landlord) and much of the rates on their home.

The rules for all these benefits are pitched mainly at those who are unemployed or who are employees, but there are special rules to take account of the position of the self-employed. If your income is low, and you think you might be entitled to claim, find out more by asking for advice from your local Citizen's Advice Bureau or, if there is one, a local Welfare Rights Centre or Law Centre. All these advisers are trained to deal with social security matters. Don't be one of those who does not ask for, and therefore does not get, their entitlement. It is believed there are many thousands of self-employed people who are entitled, particularly, to family credit, but who don't claim it because they don't know about it.

Planning your own future benefits

First, the bad news. Retirement pensions are not very good and are getting steadily worse. That's not intended as a political statement, it's a fact of life which no political party of any kind can wish away. The reason is simple, and all around you. There are fewer young people entering the job market every year, and there are more people retiring and living to a considerable age.

The arithmetic of that is unavoidable, and effects every one of us. There will be fewer people around working, and they will have to pay more out to pensioners. This is because the state NI fund is not an accumulated fund – it is a pay-as-you-go scheme with hardly any capital behind it. That, inevitably, means two things. Contribution rates will rise, and benefits will be cut. Both have been going on steadily over the last 15 years, and will go on happening. Whether you are planning to retire in the near future or far future, take steps to protect your own position and that of the family whilst you can afford to do so.

Tax help in planning

There is an additional reason why you should plan ahead. If you invest your income in the right way you will get help in the shape of tax reliefs from the Government to assist you in doing so.

You cannot afford it? That is a common reaction. The truth is that you cannot afford not to, if you have any reasonable level of income at all and you do plan, as I do, to retire. After all, you are paying other people's pension contributions every time you buy a train ticket or pay your rates. Indeed, some of the royalties from this book are going into paying for my retirement! So why not yours?

There has for many years been tax help for the self-employed in building up provision for retirement or – and you need to think of this too – benefits for the widow and family left when someone dies. Ask yourself this question if you have a family – what would they live on if you were killed this morning? They may be entitled to the benefits listed above, but is that good enough? And don't put off the answer. An old friend and neighbour of mine died without warning yesterday morning – not that much older than me. What is your answer? Then do something about it.

Personal pensions

Help comes, from 1988, in the form of a **personal pension** for yourself and your dependents. A personal pension scheme must be in a form approved by the tax authorities, but in practice standard schemes offered by the main companies will be approved. Tax relief comes two ways: an allowed deduction by you of premiums against your profits before tax, and an exemption of the funds of the pension company from either income tax or CGT (or their corporation tax equivalents) whilst the funds are held for you. You pay tax only when you draw the pension. Even then, you can receive a tax-free lump sum instead of part of your pension.

Tax relief for premiums

The amount of tax relief you can claim against your profits depends on your age. The maximum is as follows:

Age	Percentage of income
Up to 51	17.5%
51–55	20%
56–60	22.5%
61 or older	27.5%

That relief can be claimed each year, but can also be set off against earlier income if you did not claim the full benefit in the previous year. Experts agree that, especially when you are near to retirement, you should be using your allowance as fully as you can afford, including unused allowances from past years.

In addition to that, you can claim a deduction of up to 5% or your profits for a scheme to provide benefits for your dependants (your husband or wife, and your dependant children) on your death.

Get the experts in

Pension contributions are a trade-off: income now or income then. How you should best make that trade-off is a matter on which you should seek advice. As a starter, read one of the companion books to this, *Planning your pension* (published by *Longman* as part of the *Allied Dunbar Money Guide* series), so you make the best use of the tax break provided. Then get the experts in. Ask pension and insurance companies, or brokers, for some quotes and examples of the ways in which you could be planning ahead. If your business is worth quite a bit, you should be planning this along with other plans to deal with retirement and tax. We deal with that in Chapter 12.

10 Joining the VAT race

The whole world, it seems, is joining the VAT race and adopting value added tax as the way to tax sales. We started in 1973 when we joined the European Communities (the Common Market). VAT can now be found throughout Europe, and in every other part of the world. In other words, if you are in business, you have to join the VAT race. It isn't about to go away.

VAT is proving so popular partly (surprise, surprise!) because it can raise a lot of money at what seems a fairly low rate of tax. It is also because the idea of VAT is simple and fair (even if the reality seems something other!). Every time a supply of either goods or services is made, the supplier (unless selling at below cost), will be **adding value** to what is supplied. If the supply is covered by VAT, tax must be added at a set percentage of the total sale price, so including the added value. The example on page 123 demonstrates this.

VAT information

The VAT Office are good at producing detailed guidance for those caught in the VAT race. Some of this guidance is compulsory – you must follow the details laid down. This is usually set out in official Notices. Other guidance is to help and explain, in pamphlet form. If you are likely to be involved, get the following:

The VAT Guide (Notice 700) – this is a must!
VAT: Retail Schemes (Notice 727) – also a must if you are
selling goods direct to the public.
Cash Accounting (Notice 731) – this is explained below.
Filling in your VAT return
Keeping records and accounts
The Ins and Outs of VAT.

Those, and other leaflets on detailed topics, are yours for
the asking (there are a whole lot more, eg on second hand
ships and shoes, though not apparently sealing wax and
cabbages – all listed in *The VAT Guide*). For that reason, this
chapter need not go into great detail. It explains how VAT
works and draws attention to some problems.

Ins and outs

VAT is a tax of ins and outs, but just to confuse you the outs
are referred to as inputs and the ins as outputs. Let me explain.
Whenever a registered person makes a supply which is
VATable, VAT must be added to the bill and collected by
the supplier. This tax is known as **output tax,** although it is,
of course, income. Whenever the supplier pays a bill for
goods or services, he or she will pay VAT on that bill. This
VAT is called **input tax,** although it is an outgoing. Whoever
invented the phraseology for VAT clearly intended it to be
different from income tax – but did they have to make up
a whole new language?

All this talk of inputs and outputs is because it is the job of
all registered businesses to account to the VAT Office for the
difference between output tax and input tax, that is, between
tax collected and tax paid. That difference will, as the
example shows, amount to a tax on the value added to supplies
by the supplier.

Becoming a VAT collector

VAT does not apply to everything sold or supplied. In particular, it does not apply to a supply by a private person. The law provides that VAT may only be collected by a person who is a **taxable person**. To be a taxable person, the individual or company must be carrying on a business where the turnover of the total of all business dealings exceeds set limits. These limits (which vary every year) are set out in the box below.

EXAMPLE

How VAT works

Al runs a business producing hand-embroidered material. Unknown to Al, Beth buys Al's products to make 'folk' costumes. Beth sells folk costumes to Cath, a clothing wholesaler. Don is one of Cath's retailer customers, and he buys a particular folk cardigan which Ed recently bought from Don's shop for £120.

At each stage of this chain, the supplier is in business, and makes a **standard-rated** supply for VAT purposes. That is, the seller adds 15% VAT to the selling price. But at each stage, the VAT Office only collect the VAT on the value added at *that* stage. Here's how it happens.

Stage 1:
Al sells material to Beth for £15 plus VAT (a price of £17.25). For simplicity's sake, assume Al paid nothing for the thread and other stuff used in the material. Al will collect the £2.25 VAT and pay it to the VAT Office.

Stage 2:
Beth makes the cardigan, and sells it to Cath for £40 plus VAT (a total of £46). Beth collects £6 VAT, but can recoup the £2.25 VAT she paid Al from this. She pays the VAT Office the difference, £3.75.

Stage 3:
Cath sells the cardigan to Don for £60 plus VAT, a total of £69. Don collects £9 VAT, but spent £6 on the cardigan, which he recoups, sending £3 to the VAT Office.

Stage 4:
Don sells the cardigan to ed for £120. Don does not add VAT to his prices, so he has to pay the VAT Office out of the £120. For VAT purposes, he is treated as selling the cardigan to Ed for the sum which, when he adds VAT at 15%, gives the total of £120. This works out at £104.35, plus VAT of £15.65. Don will pay the £15.65, less the £9 he paid, to the VAT Office.

How the VAT was paid
Ed paid a total of £15.65 on the cardigan, and the VAT Office collected that much – but not from Ed. Instead they were paid: £2.25 by Al, £3.75 by Beth, £3 by Cath, and £6.65 by Don. Each has therefore paid the VAT Office tax on the amount of value added by her or him (that is the amount spent on improving or selling on the product, plus the profit made in doing so).

When you have to register for VAT: the 1988–89 figures

You must register for VAT within one month of your turnover exceeding, or being predicted to exceed, any of these three limits:

- total turnover over the last 12 months of at least £22,100
- total turnover over the last three months of at least £7,500, or
- predicted turnover over the next 12 months of at least £22,100.

The 12 and three month periods are any period of 12 or three months ending on 31 March, 30 June, 30 September or 31 December. For figures for other years ask the VAT Office for their free leaflet *Should I be registered for VAT?*

These figures are total **turnover**, not the profits. You are still liable to register for VAT even though you are making a loss, once the total turnover on any business you are carrying on exceed these limits.

Turnover must include all the businesses you carry on. For instance, if your main business is an antique shop, but you also regularly write articles for magazines, you must include both the shop profits and the article fees in your turnover. It will not include businesses run by others (although the VAT office have powers to stop fiddling by splitting up a business between different people). If you write the articles, but the antique shop is run by your wife, or by a partnership of you and your wife, the shop and your writing have to be looked at separately to see if both or either must register.

It is vitally important that, if your business does exceed these figures, you register for VAT as soon as possible. If you do not, you are still liable for the tax – and may incur stiff penalties in addition.

What if I don't have to register?

You have the right to register voluntarily, even if you are not required to do so, if you are carrying on business at a lower level of turnover, or if you are intending to carry on a business, but are only just getting started. It may be an advantage to register even if you do not have to do so for a number of reasons. First, you may not wish people to know that your turnover is less than the set figures. Another reason is to claim back VAT paid as soon as possible if the business will have to be registered anyway. Again, if you are not sure if the business will end up making a profit or achieving the turnover levels, it may be better to get the VAT back at the beginning.

How to register

If you think you must register, contact your local VAT Office of Customs and Excise straight away. They will, if asked, let you have a VAT Pack, consisting of:

The registration form (VAT 1)
A booklet: *Should I be registered for VAT?*
A booklet: *VAT Trade Classification*
Other information leaflets

For a copy of VAT 1, see the end of this book. All that the VAT Office really need is your name, trading address, and a few basic details about the size and kind of business. It must be returned to the VAT Office nearest your business address (for the address of a VAT Office, look in your local phone book under Customs and Excise).

What happens after registration?

Once registered, you must charge VAT on all supplies made by you which are **standard-rated**. You must also keep full records of your business, and make regular returns to the VAT Office on the income and outgoings of your business. With each return, you send a cheque for the VAT collected by you, less the VAT paid out by you, during that period. You must also give a proper VAT invoice to anyone asking for it whenever you charge VAT on a supply.

You supply goods or services any time you sell, exchange or give something to someone else as part of your business. For most purposes whether the 'something' is goods or services (or some of both together) does not matter. It is chiefly of concern when dealing with exports or imports, or – when a VAT rate changes – working out precisely when a supply was made. Normally, these points don't cause problems. But you do have to check whether VAT does or does not attach to every single sale or other supply (such as giving goods or meals to employees or Christmas presents to business friends).

If not registered, you must not add VAT to a bill. To do so is a criminal offence, and the VAT Office can collect the tax from you if they catch you doing it, but will not allow you any deductions.

VAT rates and supplies

There are three ways in which supplies are treated for VAT purposes:

- *Zero-rate supplies* – some kinds of supply are technically charged to VAT, but at a 0% rate of tax. This means the seller adds no VAT to the bill when making a supply, but can claim back any input tax paid out in making the supply (for example, on petrol or telephones). These are listed below.
- *Exempt supplies* – these are supplies on which the supplier cannot charge VAT, and also cannot claim back any VAT incurred in making the supply. A list is set out below.
- *Standard-rated supplies* – any supply which is neither zero-rated nor exempt is a standard-rated supply. If a supply is standard-rated, the supplier must add VAT at 15% (the current standard rate) to the price when making the supply. This covers everything not in the two lists which follow.

Zero-rated supplies

The following goods and services are currently zero-rated:

- *Aircraft and air services*, including selling and maintaining aircraft, passenger and freight transport by air, airport and other incidental charges
- *Animal food stuffs*, but not pet foods
- *Books, magazines, newspapers*, maps and leaflets, and also news services supplied to newspapers or the public
- *Caravans and houseboats* designed to be lived in permanently
- *Charity supplies* including supplies by them, eg through a charity shop, and some supplies to them – this also covers some supplies to the NHS
- *Children's clothing*
- *Coal*, coke and other solid fuels
- *Construction and demolition work* charged on buildings (but not repairs or alterations, except to listed buildings) including

architects, surveyors, and engineers fees, and also fixtures
normally supplied in buildings (but these rules are to change in
1989)

- **Drinks** (tea, coffee, etc) other than:
  Alcoholic drinks
  Fizzy drinks like lemonade
  Fruit juices
  Mineral waters
- **Electricity**
- **Exports of goods** (goods are charged when they are imported to
  the country where they will be finally sold)
- **Food** sold for human consumption (and not supplied to be eaten
  immediately), but the following are standard rated
  Chocolates, sweets and confectionery
  Ice cream and lollies and their ingredients
  Potato crisps and similar products
  Salted roasted nuts and other savoury snacks
- **Freight transport overseas**
- **Fuel oils**, and kerosene, but not petrol, diesel or fuels for
  transport use
- **Gas**
- **International services** – the rules here are quite complicated. If
  supplying services outside the UK, check the position carefully.
- **Medicines** supplied on prescription, and many kinds of supply
  made to handicapped or blind people
- **New buildings** sold, or leased for over 21 years, by the builders
  (but these rules will be changed in 1989)
- **Passenger transport** by rail, coach, bus and other vehicles
  carrying 12 or more passengers, but not taxis or cars
- **Protective boots and helmets** sold to employees
- **Ships and shipping services**, including selling and servicing
  ships, passenger and freight transport and port charges
- **Take-away food** supplied cold (eg sandwiches)
- **Water rates** and charges, including sewerage charges

Exempt supplies

The following supplies are currently exempted:

- **Bank and building society** current, deposit and savings accounts
  (see also **Credit**)
- **Betting and gaming**
- **Credit facilities** including making advances and loans, hire

purchase agreements and issuing debentures and similar securities
- **Education and training** by schools or universities, or similar services to them not made for profit
- **Funerals**, burials and cremations
- **Health services** provided by doctors, dentists, opticians, nurses, pharmacists and the supplementary medical professions
- **Insurance** and the work of agents and brokers related to insurance claims
- **Heritage property** such as works of art given special tax status for inheritance tax and CGT
- **Land and building sales** and the sale or letting of any right to use land or buildings, but not for camping, parking, fishing, shooting, storing boats or aircraft, holding sports or exhibitions, or for holiday accommodation or for hotel or similar services (but there will be some changes to this in 1989)
- **Lotteries**
- **Postal services** supplied by the Post Office
- **Professional, pressure group and trade associations** supplies to members
- **Sports competitions** entry rights (but not charges for entering or using premises)
- **Tenancy agreements**, except holiday lettings or hotel or similar residential accommodation (but there will be changes to this in 1989)
- **Trade union** supplies to members
- **Welfare services** and goods supplied by charities and public bodies, but not for profit

How to charge VAT

If making a standard-rate supply, add VAT at 15% to the bill. Alternatively, you can choose not to add VAT to the bill, but can treat part of the price paid as the VAT (as Don did in the example at the beginning of the chapter). What you can't do legally is quote a price without mentioning VAT in any way, and then afterwards claim that the price is VAT-exclusive so VAT has to be added, unless it is clearly understood (for example because of previous dealings with that customer) that prices are VAT-exclusive. If you advertise or quote VAT-exclusive prices, put up a notice, or print a clause in your terms, saying so. Otherwise you may commit an offence under the Trades Descriptions or other consumer protection legislation.

When to charge VAT

First, some more jargon. Ever had a **tax point**? No, it's not a thing to argue about, it's the technical term for the time at which VAT must be charged on a supply. There are quite complicated rules about this, but in summary, the position is:

- *Goods* – the tax point is the earliest of the date when the goods are removed from the supplier's premises, the date when the goods are paid for, or the date when a **tax invoice** is sent out by the supplier. In practice, if a tax invoice is issued within 14 days after the goods are physically supplied to the customer (or the customer pays, if earlier), then the date of issue of the invoice is the tax point.
- *Services* – the tax point is the date when you have finished performing the services being supplied (except, of course, for sending out the bill!). Again, if the invoice is sent out within 14 days of that day, the date of the invoice is taken.

15% of what?

Of the amount included in the tax invoice, is the answer in most cases. If you make a supply, you must account for VAT even if you choose not to send out an invoice (for example, where you have supplied goods free to an employee as a present). In tricky cases such as this – or where you are selling cheap for non-commercial reasons (to a friend for example) – you should charge the VAT on the market value of the supply.

Discounts cause problems. The rules say that if you offer a customer a discount, and the discounted price is paid, VAT is charged only on the discounted price. This is also true where you set a price for a supply, but then reduce it for prompt payment, even if the customer pays late and so does not get the discount. Discounts that are left open (eg, 'if you find the goods sold cheaper elsewhere in town this week, we will refund the difference') are to be ignored.

Problems are frequently caused because a supply is made up of several things, eg a mail-order supply will cover not just the goods, but also packaging and postal charges, and possibly credit charges too. Where the additional supplies, such as packaging, are incidental, and there is no separate charge, the whole supply is treated as the supply of the main item only. But where there is a separate charge for postage, or where there is an unusual amount of packing, the supply has to be treated as a **mixed supply**.

The amount paid for **mixed** supplies, that is, supplies of two or more separate goods or services together, has to be split up so that the VAT can be applied separately to each part of the supply. Even if a supply does not have to be split up, you can sometimes split it yourself to the same effect. For example, if you supply goods under a credit sale to a customer who is paying for the finance in addition to the purchase price of the goods, you are making two supplies: the goods, probably standard-rated, and the credit, which is exempt. If you charge the two together without separating the finance charge, you must charge VAT on the lot.

Tax invoices

Yet more jargon. A **tax invoice** is the document you are
required to issue when making a supply of an item within
the scope of VAT, that is, your customer is also a VAT-
registered business. That means all businesses will need to
have forms of VAT invoice available. To comply with the
law, the invoices must set out required information to allow
the customer to claim the tax in the invoice, and for the VAT
authorities to check.

A simple form of invoice can be used where the total amount
(including the tax) is not over £50. For transactions over £50,
a full VAT invoice must be given. The diagrams on pages
134 and 135 show what the two must contain.

Keeping records

By now it will be clear that VAT is an invoice-based tax, or
put another way, a paper-pusher's paradise. Everything coming
into the business has its output tax attached (it's a jargon-
lover's paradise as well!), and the output tax has a tax invoice
attached. The same with all the business's expenditure. This
will have input tax, and therefore a tax invoice, attached.
Your job is very simple – just to keep track of every single
tax invoice. More than this, you must by law keep a check
on every supply made by your business, including all the
exempt and zero-rated supplies.

Put that way, it sounds horrific. It is not easy to meet all the
VAT requirements, but, as I stressed in *Running your own
business*, a business which does not have proper and full
records is inviting trouble in the longer term. VAT officials
may well be doing you a favour by forcing you to do this.
Where this level of bureaucracy (imposed or self-imposed)

can become a burden is the retail trade, but there are **Special Schemes** operating there which make life simpler. The other problem of an invoice-based tax is that you must account for tax charged on an invoice even though your customer has not paid. This is tough on the smaller business, but the problem is now eased by the new **cash accounting scheme**.

Special schemes for retailers

Formal details of the special schemes available are given in VAT Notice 727, *Retail schemes* (last revised 1987). An explanation of each scheme is given in *Choosing your retail scheme*, and details of each scheme are given in a series of *How to work. . .* pamphlets. If engaged or to be engaged in a retail trade, obtain these from your local VAT Office.

There are 14 different schemes or variants of schemes designed to simplify the process of finding how much VAT your business is collecting and incurring. They have different turnover levels (and therefore can require different levels of detail) and take into account whether your business supplies goods only of one kind (eg just zero-rated), or of two or three kinds, and the proportions of the different kinds of supply.

For example, Scheme C applies to businesses with a total turnover of under £90,000 in a year which is supplying both zero-rated and standard-rated goods. Instead of invoicing every transaction, the supplier works out the VAT by applying a standard mark-up, set by the VAT Office, to his or her purchases of standard-rated goods (so only needs to keep the invoices for purchases). That example shows that retail schemes can save a lot of time and should be investigated by any retailer.

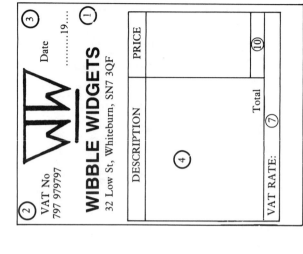

Simple form of VAT invoice
(supplies under £50)

Your invoices must include

1 Your name and address
2 Your VAT number
3 Taxpoint (time of supply)
4 Description identifying
   goods/services supplied
   including
5 quantity and charge
6 cash discounts, if any
7 VAT rate
8 Total charge, excluding VAT
9 Total VAT payable
10 Total charge, including VAT
11 Customer's name and address
12 Identification number

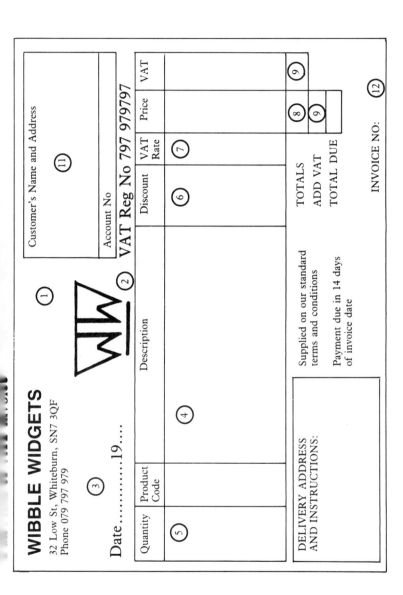

Cash accounting

This is a recent simplification of VAT available to smaller businesses. Full details are contained in VAT Notice 731, *Cash Accounting*. Cash accounting can be used by any business which has taxable supplies of under £250,000 in any year, and which has its VAT affairs up to date, unless it is already using a retail scheme.

The point of the cash accounting scheme is to allow the business to get away from the fact that under the normal scheme the business is treated as collecting and paying tax whenever invoices are issued (because of the rules on **tax point**). This can mean that the business is accounting to the VAT Office for tax not yet collected. To avoid this, the business is allowed to make returns on the basis of tax on payments received less tax on payments made. This will be of advantage to any business suffering from slow payers and the occasional bad debt. It will not be of advantage to a business which pays more VAT than it collects (eg where all or most of the supplies are zero-rated) or where supplies are paid for at the time (as in a shop not allowing credit). The cash accounting scheme does not cut down on the record-keeping.

Annual accounting

Another new scheme (scheduled to start in July 1988) does allow simpler bookkeeping. Businesses eligible for cash accounting will also qualify to make annual VAT returns instead of quarterly. At the time of writing rules for this scheme were still being finalised.

11 A tax on your premises

I can't remember who first said 'Buy land – they don't make it any more'. Does it matter? The advice is just as good whoever gave it. There's another truism that goes along with the first: 'Tax land – they can't pretend it's not there.' Much of our history reflects the way people have used those two bits of advice. It's no wonder that we have several taxes on land and what we do with it. That's what this chapter is about – these taxes and the practical effect to you as an owner or user of land.

Taxes on land

Most important is **rates** – the **business rates** which are to continue, and the **domestic rates** which are to be replaced by the **community charge** or poll tax. Rates are a tax on the occupation of land, and on the occupier rather than the owner. For centuries there were taxes on land ownership, but they have gone. Instead, we have an **income tax** charge on income from land (**Schedule A**), a **capital gains tax** charge on gains made from disposals of land, an **inheritance tax** charge if you make a gift of land, a **stamp duty** on the documents necessary to sell land or create leases, and **VAT** on some supplies of use of land.

The tax on land occupation

Rates are an annual charge payable to local councils (and used to finance local services). The rates charge is based on two factors:

- the **ratable value** of premises and,
- the **rate poundage** set for the year.

The rates payable on any building are the amount produced by multiplying the ratable value of that building by the rate poundage for that year. If the rate is set at, say, £2 in the £, and the ratable value of a building is £3,000, the annual rate on the building is £6,000.

How ratable value is set

It is the job of the local District Valuer's Office (DVO) of the Inland Revenue to fix the ratable value (RV) of every building in its area. These values are entered on to a public list, along with short details of the basis of the valuation. Whenever considering buying or renting premises, make sure you check the RV from the sellers or landlords (unless the rates are included in the rent). If you have any queries, check with the local DVO.

The DVO sets the RV by reference to a notional rent for the building. It is the annual rent payable for those premises, and for their current use, by a tenant who had an annual tenancy from the owner of the building under which the tenant does the repairs. However, the DVOs only revalue buildings about every 15 years (unless something has changed) so RVs are in many cases artificial. The most important point is the 'tone of the list'. By this is meant the general level of RVs in the area around a particular property. The key question is whether the RV of the individual property compares correctly with those of its neighbours.

The comparison takes into account rents actually being charged, the size of the building (to the nearest square metre), its use, levels of profits, local facilities and local problems, such as double yellow lines preventing parking or low flying aircraft overhead. It is the job of a surveyor who knows the area well to decide the correct RV for a property.

Challenging an RV

If you think an RV for premises you occupy is too high, you can challenge it. To do this, ask the local DVO for the necessary forms to get the RV reassessed. You will be asked to state an alternative RV, and give reasons why the present one is too high. It will often pay to get the experts in on this one. Choose a local professional surveyor to deal with the matter for you, and ask his advice. Before you do that, it may be useful to visit the local DVO and ask one of the staff there to explain your RV, and tell them you think it too high. Certainly when I have done that, the staff were extremely helpful.

There is a formal procedure if you challenge an RV, which gives the DVO time to make a counter-proposal. If you cannot reach agreement, the matter goes to a special local body known as the Local Valuation Court for an independent decision.

The rate poundage

Here we enter highly political territory. Local rates are currently set by each local county and district council. Because of the different policies of councils, some areas rates are much higher than others – varying in 1988 anywhere from zero to over £3 in the £. At the time of writing the government is pushing through new laws which will result in a standard national business rate. In other words the rate poundage will be the same all over the country. That means a very pleasant surprise for some and a nasty shock for others.

It will be worth watching carefully – it's already causing some strong protests.

Income tax on rents

Income tax on rents and other income from land is under **Schedule A** which applies to all UK land. It charges tax on the profits made from the land each year, less expenses. It is not used to tax trades such as market gardening, farming, mining and quarries, fisheries, ferries, or piers which exploit land or buildings – these are all handled under the Schedule D rules set out in Chapter 3. Schedule A is the landlord tax.

Furnished rents and service charges

Schedule A applies *only* to land. This means that if you let a furnished flat, or you provide both somewhere to stay and also services (such as cleaning or catering), only part of the payment made by your tenant comes under these rules.

If you impose a separate service charge that is not treated as rent. If you impose only one charge, eg, for renting a room, and the furniture in it, and as payment for services, the charge must be split between the various things it covers for tax purposes. The non-rent payments are either trading income, or are treated the same way (so the deductions rules, loss rules, etc are those covered in Chapters 3 and 4). This applies to **holiday lets** which are treated under special provisions just like trading income.

If you have income from a furnished let, you can tell the Tax Inspector that you want the whole lot treated under the non-land rules. This is worth doing if your expenses are greater than your income, so you can set the loss against any other similar income.

Allowable expenses

The only expenses deductible from rents received when working out the profit under the Schedule A rules are revenue expenses of approved kinds. Capital expenditure (for example, on improving a building) is not allowable – instead it can be set off against the sale proceeds of the building for capital gains tax purposes. There are limited exceptions to this general rule, when capital allowances are available for expenditure on land or buildings. See Chapter 5.

The following revenue expenses may be deducted:

- maintenance and repairs costs (but not costs of improvements)
- buildings insurance premiums
- management expenses (eg on collecting rents or legal fees for a new tenancy agreement)
- rates and water rates, when paid by the landlord
- rentcharges, ground or other rent paid by the landlord
- expenses incurred in providing services to tenants under leases for which they make no separate rent payment (eg maintaining the garden without separate cost to tenants).

If levying a service charge, you can deduct any of the forms of expenditure mentioned in Chapter 4, provided that the expense is incurred for the purpose of earning the profits on that business. If you are letting furnished property, one deduction that is claimable is a reasonable allowance for wear and tear on the furniture.

Furnished holiday lets

Technically, running furnished holiday lettings is not a business, and the income is charged partly under Schedule A and partly under the parallel rules of Schedule D Case VI that apply to furnished lets instead of the trading income rules. To avoid injustice, however, a person whose income comes from holiday lettings is treated as if he or she is trading for the purpose of claiming tax reliefs, such as the CGT relief when retiring.

Rent or buy?

Tax rules may make a difference to the decision whether you rent premises for your business or buy them. If you rent, the full cost of the rent is a deductible expense for income tax purposes. If you buy, you can claim deduction for interest payments on the money borrowed (if any) to make the purchase. You may be able to claim capital allowances in some cases. The **post-tax** cost is worth checking, although it will have to be weighed against other factors such as the likely increase in property prices and/or rents in the area.

How the tax is payable

Income tax on rents is collected each year on the profits of that year's rents (unlike business income which is charged on the previous year's profits). That poses a practical problem. At the time the tax is payable, you probably don't know what the profits will be. The rules get out of that one by providing that you pay tax at first on the assumption that your profits this year will be the same as those last year. The tax bill will then be adjusted at the end of the year when the actual profit is known.

If you know the income this year is going to be down on last year's, notify the Tax Inspector, giving details of the new lower rents. If you do so, the tax office will adjust the tax bill without waiting to the end of the year.

Capital payments for land

The general rule is that if you receive any capital payment for land, you may be liable to capital gains tax on it. The chief exception to this is the exemption from tax of each taxpayer's only or main residence (or home). CGT is covered in Chapter 4.

There are rules which will treat a capital sum as income to stop you avoiding income tax by receiving a sum as capital, but since 1988 you pay the same rate of tax either way, so these are now of limited practical importance in most cases, and can be ignored. There are also rules treating a **premium** paid on a lease that lasts under 50 years as being partly income. Again, these rules are now of little importance, except that where part of a premium is treated as income, it can be deducted against the trading expenses for income tax purposes.

Stamp duty on buying and selling land

If you buy or sell land, you have to use a formal document (called a deed of conveyance). If you do not use the proper formal document, the sale will be invalid. That's a good excuse for the government to impose a tax on the document, and they have done so for several hundred years. The duty is payable by the buyer.

A stamp duty is the tax you pay to have an official stamp put on your deed of conveyance. If you do not get the stamp put on the document, you cannot use the document in court – that is, you cannot enforce your rights under it. For this reason, you would be foolish not to pay the duty (as well as being liable to penalties). The stamp is put on the document by the Stamp Office of the Inland Revenue. If, as is usual, a solicitor or licenced conveyancer does the legal work for you on a purchase, it is his or her job to see this is done.

How much is the stamp duty?

There is no stamp duty if the total price for selling the land is under £30,000. If the price is £30,000 or more, the duty is 1% of the total price. The stamp is payable on the price of the land, not necessarily the total price. For example, if you are buying an office complete with full carpeting, furnishings and equipment, you should pay stamp duty only on the price of the office itself, not the additional items. For this reason, get the price split between the amount on the land, and the amount on other items. It is not worth playing clever tricks to avoid duty, for example by buying the land in several lots each costing £25,000. There are rules to prevent avoiding the duty in that way.

Gifts of land

If you make a gift of land, eg transferring the ownership of the building where the family business is carried on to your children, you may have to pay inheritance tax if you die within seven years after the gift. See Chapter 12. There may also be CGT on the gift – see also Chapter 5.

Stamp duty on renting premises

Duty is payable on any lease or agreement to lease land. It is usual to have two copies of the document – one for the landlord to keep and the other (a duplicate) for the tenant. The full stamp duty is paid on the original copy, and a fee of 50p on the duplicate.

The amount of stamp duty on a lease depends on the length of the lease, the amount of any premium or capital sum payable, and the amount of any rent. If the tenancy is for less than a year (and one year less one day is quite commonly used), and the rent is over £500, the duty is £1 (nothing if below £500). If the agreement is seven years or less, and the rent is over £500, the charge is 1% of the rent. This rises to 2% if the lease is for over seven but under 35 years, and is higher still if (unusually) the lease is over 35 years.

VAT on supplies of land and buildings

There is no VAT chargeable on private sales of land or agreements allowing use of land. Where the supply is by a business, there is still usually no VAT. Where a builder sells a building he has built, or grants a lease for over 21 years, the supply is zero-rated. Most other forms of supply of land (eg sale of land or of a building not built by the seller, or grant of a tenancy of an older building) are exempt from VAT. Taxable supplies are: providing accommodation in a hotel, boarding house or somewhere similar; providing holiday accommodation; granting rights to camp, park, shoot, fish, moor a boat, mount an exhibition or play sport – or similar activities. These rules mean in effect that those using land for a trade (eg running a car park or holiday camp) have to charge VAT, but all others do not.

VAT will become more important both on new commercial

buildings and on business tenancies in 1989. This is because the Government is going to get the law changed to extend VAT on non-domestic buildings then. However, at the time of writing, they have not announced the details of how they will do this.

12 A tax on your retirement

What is retirement age for the self-employed? One or two
people I know managed to retire before the age of 40, at
least for the first time. The oldest person was well over 90
when he stopped going into the office on a regular basis. In
both cases they were enjoying to the full the privilege of the
self-employed of working on their own terms. At the same
time too many people struggle on in self-employment long
after they wanted to retire, because they could not afford to
do so, and had not planned ahead. Will you be able to afford
to retire on the right terms?

Taxing your life's work

If your business has been at all successful, you will have built
up a reasonable amount of capital, and it will probably still be
tied up in the business. When you retire, you may want to
free some of the capital. If you do, work out the tax position.
Whether you sell the business, or just parts of it, or give it
away to members of the family, there will be tax
consequences. We must therefore look at each of the ways
you could hand the business on, and the tax effect of doing
so.

At some point, of course, the property must be handed on.
It will happen to all of us, later or sooner. I was once asked to
give an after-dinner talk to a professional audience about why
they should get their wills written right. I queried twice
whether they really wanted to talk about that after dinner,

and was assured they did. I could not, and still cannot, find any jokes to lighten the burden of such a task. I wasn't thanked then for spelling out a few home truths, and I don't expect to be thanked now. But spell them out I must. Far too many people put off sorting out their affairs, a lot of them for too long. Don't be one of them.

Leaving the business

If you are a **sole trader**, when you leave the business, the business – at least for tax purposes – ends. That is so whether you sell it, give it away or close it down. Tax consequences of ending your business need planning like any other aspect of your business.

By contrast, if your business is owned by a **company**, you are, as we saw in Chapter 6, only the owner of shares and an employee of the business. When you leave the business, it continues. It is only when the company goes out of business that the business ends.

In between those two is the position of the **partnership**. If you are in business with one or more partners, the business can come to an end every time the partnership changes. However, you can choose (provided all partners agree) that it does not end. That may be a practical solution to the problem, and many partnerships use it. But first, let's see the problem.

Income tax when the business ends

The profit charged to income tax in the year in which a business ends is not worked out on the usual **preceding year basis** (see Chapter 3). Instead, tax is based on the profits (or loss) actually made in the **income tax year** in which the business ends. That is, the profits (or loss) are worked out from 6 April to the date on which you leave the business.

As the following example shows, that can leave quite a gap between the profits taxed under the ordinary rules in the year before the end, and those profits taxed in the last year. To deal with this gap, the Revenue (but not you) may change the basis of taxing the last two full years of business on to an actual profits basis. This means they can demand that you pay tax on the profits from 6 April two years before the end of the business, until the date on which it ended, rather than the normal basis. They will do this if that increases the tax, as in the following example. Because they probably did not know when the business was going to end until after it had ended, they will raise the new tax bill after it has finished. That bill must still be paid.

EXAMPLE

What gets taxed when the business ends

Our old friend Zale ran a business for quite a few years, but sold it (at a profit) in 1988. The accounts year for the business was the calendar year, but the sale took place on 30 June 1988. What tax was payable on the profits?

As the sale occurred in June 1988, the last tax year was 1988–89, and the charge was on actual profits (which are, as in the example, usually apportioned on a month-by-month basis from the actual annual accounts). For this reason, the Revenue look again at 1987–88 and 1986–87.

Year	Agreed profits	Tax year	Taxable profits – normal rules	Taxable profits – actual basis
1985	12,000			
1986	16,000	1986–87	12,000	17,000
1987	20,000	1987–88	16,000	17,500
1988	5,000	1988–89	2,500 (½ of 5,000)	2,500

The 'actual basis' tax in 1987–88 would be ¾ of the profits for 1987, plus half the actual profits to 30 June 1988. Similarly, the actual basis in 1986–87 means ¾ of the £16,000 and the other quarter of the £20,000.

What does that mean? Zale faces an increased tax bill to pay an extra income of £5,000 in 1986–87 and of £1,500 in 1987–88. Even if Zale only pays tax at the then basic rates of income tax on those profits, there is still an extra £1,855 in income tax to pay.

Final losses

If the business ends making losses, the taxpayer may suffer the opposite problem to Zale. Instead of paying extra tax, he or she runs the danger of losing the right to get the tax **losses** against profits, and paying too much tax over the life of the business. To stop this causing too much injustice (bearing in mind the Revenue already have a choice of which years they tax near the end and go for the higher ones). there is a special tax relief. This allows traders to carry losses made in the last 12 months of business back up to three years. Had Zale made a loss in the period ending in June 1988, this would allow a reduction of profits back to 1986–87.

Other income tax problems at close

Another issue to be sorted out is what happens to capital allowances. Each item of **plant and machinery**, or **industrial building** or other asset on which allowances have been granted, must be re-assessed and made subject to a **balancing charge** or **balancing allowance**. What happens depends on what is done with the plant. If sold, there may be extra tax to pay in the form of a balancing allowance if the amount made on selling the equipment exceeds the unallowed tax relief on buying it. If scrapped, there will probably be a balancing allowance. If used privately (for example, the business van becomes the family car) it will be treated as being sold at its market value, as it will if it is given away. That may result in a balancing charge.

Trading stock must be valued at open market value at close. This may be higher than the value used in the accounts till then (which may be lower of cost and market). Any profit element 'hidden' in the stock will now bear tax. If stock is turned over to private use, it is treated as being sold at market value. If disposed of cheap in a closing sale, the proceeds will be the market value.

Paying VAT when the business ends

The VAT rules make it clear that you are running your business for VAT purposes even when you are disposing of it. A sale or gift of business equipment is a **supply** of goods and must bear standard-rate VAT when that is appropriate, even though it is in effect a sale of part of the business. Further, the sale or gift of the business as a going concern is expressly made a supply 'in the furtherance of a business', and is therefore VATable.

Once you have sold or disposed of the business, you must deregister, unless you are carrying on, or intend to carry on, some other business which will also bring you into the scope of registration. Notice must be given within 30 days of the business ending.

Remember that you have to account to the VAT Office for all VAT. If you are one of those managing to keep a cash-float in the business based on VAT collected and not yet paid to Customs and Excise, that will come to an end.

Taxing the sale

If you sell the business or its assets, there is a potential **capital gains tax** charge on top of the income tax. The sale will be a disposal for CGT purposes, so you need to work out the gain. As we saw in Chapter 5, that gain is made larger because any **roll-over reliefs** you have come to an end. This is because where you postponed paying tax on assets sold and replaced during the life of the business, the value of the new asset was reduced, possibly back to 1982 values.

CGT applies to sale proceeds of land and buildings, goodwill, industrial or intellectual property (such as sale of a trademark), and any other assets except wasting and exempt assets. Remember that plant and machinery on which you received capital allowances is included only if you sell at above the original cost price – so you cannot claim losses on their sale. But you may have roll-over relief on those assets and end with CGT gains though real losses.

If, when all is added together, you show a profit (and, tax apart, I hope you do!), you must pay CGT unless retirement relief helps you out.

CGT retirement relief

If you are over 60 when you sell the business (or, if under 60, are retiring because of ill-health), check how far the retirement relief can – or, if you changed things round a bit, could – help. If you worked full-time with the business, and it is your business or one owned by a company of which you own a lot of shares, there is a generous level of relief. At maximum, this removes entirely the CGT on the first £125,000 of gains, and reduces to half the tax payable on the rest up to £500,000. But if you sell at 59, or if you fail to meet the requirements, you will lose all or part of that valuable relief. More details are set out in the box, so keep an eye on them.

Getting relief from gains tax on retirement

You must be:

- 60 or over, or
- have retired on ill-health grounds and be disposing of the business, or business assets, or shares in the company owning the business.

If you own the business direct, you must have done so for at least one year prior to selling (when you will get 10% of the maximum relief), and you must have owned it for a minimum of ten years to get full relief.

If you are a partner in a partnership running the business, and you retire from the partnership, you can claim relief as if your partnership interest were business assets.

If your business is owned by a family company (or group of companies) which is a trading company (or group), you can claim the relief if you have been a full-time working director of the company, and the company is either one where you have 25% or more of the voting power, or your family has over 50% of the voting control and you have at least 5%. (There are complex provisions dealing with groups of companies and family trusts – in any case like that you need expert advice.)

Passing on the business by gift

If you make a gift of business assets of a business carried on by you or of shares in your family company which is a trading company, and retirement relief is not available, you can still postpone a charge to tax on the gift. The relief will also apply if you sell the business at an undervalue. Relief is granted by treating the disposal as happening on a **no-gain/no-loss** basis, with the recipient receiving the gift not at market value, but at the no-gain/no-loss value (ie what you paid for the assets or the value at which you were given them).

To get the relief it must be claimed by both you and the person receiving the assets.

Stamp duty

If you sell land (or other assets using a deed) stamp duty is payable at 1% of the capital value of the property transferred, payable by the buyer. If you make a gift by deed no stamp duty is payable.

Death duties and wills

We have had death duties in this country for centuries, but they keep changing their names, as Chancellors like to seem to be reforming them. Until 1974 we had an estate duty, but then it became capital transfer tax, only to be changed in 1984 back to estate duty, but this time called inheritance tax. The trouble is that a lot of people, if they ever do write a will, tend to leave it unreviewed for years – whilst politicians seem unable to leave the taxes that apply to wills alone. If you made a will some time ago – and you should have done – check it is still appropriate. 1988 has seen some major changes in thinking amongst tax advisers on **estate planning** – the handling of your property to avoid excess tax – so now is a good time to review things. Property can be handed on in two ways – by a lifetime gift (the jargon is still in Latin: *inter vivos*), or on death. Where are the tax problems?

When inheritance tax has to be paid

Inheritance tax (IHT) is payable on any transfer by an individual to another individual (or to a trust) which is not a market value transfer (ie part at least is a gift), where that transfer happens:

- on the death of the transferor, or
- within seven years before the death.

unless in either case the transfer is exempt from IHT. IHT does not apply to companies (except for anti-avoidance provisions aimed at small companies making gifts on behalf of individuals). It applies to gifts through settlements, but these are beyond the scope of this book.

The amount of IHT to be paid

IHT works on the basis of adding up all the transfers within the scope of the tax, that is, all transfers made by the transferor within seven years of death, together with the total value of taxable property in the transferor's estate at death. No IHT is payable up to a maximum amount. Once the total of gifts and property in the estate exceeds that amount, tax is payable on the excess at the rates applying that year. The current rates are given in the box.

Rates of inheritance tax: 1988–89

No tax is payable until the total of transfers reaches **£110,000**. Above that level, the excess value is taxable at **40%**.

Who pays IHT?

IHT payable on a gift within seven years of death is payable by the recipient out of the gift. IHT payable on an estate is paid by the executors or personal representatives, and it is their job to share the tax out amongst the beneficiaries. If there is a will, they must follow instructions in the will about who pays. This needs watching when writing a will. For instance, if Aunt Agatha wants to leave all her shares in Agatha's Cookies Ltd to nephew Neil, is he going to pay the IHT on the shares, or is someone else (and if so, who)? Can Neil afford to pay, or is he going to be forced to sell something to finance getting the shares? Should this be paid for by a life assurance policy bought by Agatha for the purpose?

IHT and gifts

For IHT purposes, any large gift which is not exempt is a gamble. If the transferor dies within seven years of the date on which the gift is made, the value of the gift is added to the value of any property the transfer leaves on her or his death in calculating IHT liability. This does not apply to exempt gifts (see box).

Planning for IHT

Points to watch in planning to reduce IHT liability:
- while there is always a risk that there will be IHT to pay on a larger gift, the younger the transferor the lower the risk
- make gifts of assets that are going to rise in value, and hang on to those which will not
- it pays to use the exempt forms of transfer as far as appropriate, as there is no IHT on these
- it may be wise to ensure that cash is available to pay any IHT that becomes due, for example by insuring the life of the

transferor by a suitable life assurance policy made in favour of the transferee
- the form of the gift should be such as to reduce the amount of the gift for tax purposes (eg using exemptions).

Remember that although a transfer may be exempt from IHT, or the tax liability is reduced for IHT purposes, the gift will be separately taxable as a disposal of assets for CGT purposes. Each tax operates independently of the others.

Gifts exempted from IHT

No IHT is payable on a lifetime transfer of any of the following kinds:

- transfers to the husband or wife of the transferor (unless he or she is based overseas) (also no CGT)
- wedding gifts to children (up to £5,000), to grandchildren (up to £2,500) or others (up to £1,000)
- the first £3,000 a year of gifts by any transferor
- small gifts of £250 or less to any one recipient in any year
- gifts to charities (also no CGT)
- gifts of heritage property (such as works of art of special value) approved by the relevant Treasury committee (also no CGT)
- gifts to political parties
- gifts totalling in all less than the maximum level of the nil rate band of the tax (see above)

Relief on gifts three or more years before death

If the transferor dies more than three years after the date of the gift, but less than seven years later, only part of the tax charge on the transfer is made. How much is shown in the following table:

Period between *gift and death*	*Percentage reduction* *of tax otherwise charged*
3–4 years	20%
4–5 years	40%
5–6 years	60%
6–7 years	80%

If, for example, the transferor dies 6½ years after making the gift, the amount of tax payable on the gift will be only one-fifth of that payable had the gift been made on death. Gifts within three years of death bear full tax.

Relief on transfers of business property

Separately from the reliefs already mentioned, special reliefs operate to protect any gift or transfer of business property from the full rate of tax. If the transfer is of a business, or an interest in a business, relief of 50% is given against the value of the property transferred (that is, a transfer of £50,000 is treated as being only £25,000). The same level of relief applies where the transfer is of shares giving the transferor control of a company running a business, or of unquoted shares where the transferor did not have control but is transferring at least 25% of the shares.

In other cases, such as a smaller holding of shares, or assets used by a partnership of which the transferor is a partner, or used by a company of which the trustee is a controlling shareholder, relief is only 30% of the value.

Relief at 50% is also available for transfers of **agricultural land** transferred with vacant possession. If the land is subject to a tenancy, the relief is 30%.

Death and taxes

. . . as the saying goes, are the only two certainties. When someone dies, her or his estate must be transferred according to law to the beneficiaries. This amounts, in effect, to a disposal in the capital gains tax sense, but no capital gains tax is payable on a transfer of property on death. Instead, the beneficiaries are treated as receiving the property at its market value at the time of the death without any CGT being payable. There is also no stamp duty on transfers made because of a death.

Because of these exemptions, the only tax payable on death is IHT. This is payable, as we noted above, on the total value of both the estate and gifts made within the previous seven years. However, just as there are gifts exempted from, or partly relieved from IHT, so some gifts are exempt when made on death.

The beneficiaries on death are those people named in the will of the person who died, assuming he or she made a will (which should always be done). If no will has been made – which is the case surprisingly often – the property is transferred under the intestacy rules laid down by law. Only if there is a will can any systematic advantage be made of the IHT exemptions.

Valuing an estate

For IHT purposes, the value of the estate left on someone's death includes everything that belongs to the person who has died, plus all property that comes into the estate because of the death, less most debts, the cost of the funeral, and any reductions in the value of the estate caused by the death.

Do you know what your estate would be worth, were anything to happen to you now? There will be your share in the home (is it jointly owned by both husband and wife, or just one of you); your business or your share of it (noting that the value is reduced for IHT purposes by the business property relief – the business itself may go down in value when the owner dies if the business depends heavily on the personality of its owner because of loss of goodwill); your bank and building society deposits, shares and other savings; any life policies which you took out and belong to the estate; any damages due to the estate if, for example, your death was caused by a negligent motorist, and similarly any insurance payments.

Legacies exempt from IHT

Property left on death is exempt in the following cases:

- all transfers to the widow or widower (unless based abroad)
- all transfers to charities, political parties or of heritage property.

The reliefs for business property also apply to transfers on death.

Why you need to plan

Passing on your business to the family therefore involves a web of complications from income tax, capital gains tax, VAT, stamp duty and IHT. If you sell, there will be no IHT, and the buyer will pay the stamp duty, but it will make the CGT much harder to avoid if you are under 60. If you give it away now, you can postpone the CGT and run the risk of IHT, whereas if you leave it to pass after you die, there will be IHT, but CGT is avoided. Now that the tax problems have been outlined, your task is to think through how best to put your own plans for retirement, and to protect your business if you should die, into effect. The worst plan is no plan.

Get your will written

There should be a number of parts to your plan. First, get a proper will written for yourself, and review it from time to time. When you are younger, if married and bringing up children, the best will may be a simple one – just transferring the property to your husband or wife. But is that enough? What if, to think the unthinkable, your husband or wife (or anyone else to whom you leave something) dies at the same time as you, or just a little later? One problem is that this situation could make two lots of tax payable (although there is tax relief to stop a full charge to tax where property passes on the death of two separate people in quick succession). If the transfer is to your husband or wife, the IHT exemption may fail to work. What reserve provisions do you need? It is this sort of problem which needs professional help – get in the experts; see your solicitors.

Using trusts

We have largely ignored trusts in this book, but it is worth mentioning here that a trust may be an unavoidable answer if when you die the property must pass to your children, and they, or some of them, are under 18. A solicitor should be able to advise on how to combine dealing with these various possibilities with the minimum IHT. There are tricky issues if, for example, you business as a sole trader has to be handed on to people too young to run it. The answer may be a trading trust – but who should the trustees be?

Another part of your planning should be lifetime transfers. If you are happily married, would it be wise to make sure that your property is held between you in roughly equal shares. There is no tax of any kind on a transfer from husband to wife (or the other way round).

Making the right gifts

Should you start handing on part of the business to other members of the family, a bit at a time, now? The rules about exemptions, combined with the amount that can be transferred without paying tax, mean that considerable amounts of property can be transferred free of IHT. Generally, the first £3,000 every year is free of IHT, and you can transfer another £110,000 every seven years tax free as well – an average of a further £15,000 a year. It is not easy to transfer a business you own outright in bits to take advantage of this. It is easier if the business is owned by a company or, in some cases, if settlements are used. Or you can do it by taking out a life policy, making a gift of it to the family (so nothing comes into your estate on death), but continuing to pay the premiums yourself. Again, expert advice in this area will probably be wise.

13 When to pay

When you pay tax can sometimes be as important as how much you pay. Your planning should take account of both – it helps you watch your flow if you take full account of the timing of tax payments and allowances. As you will expect by now, there is no consistent set of rules about this. Linked in with when to pay is the question of how the taxfolk decide how much is to be paid, and your rights to object. That's what we look at in the next chapter.

How you pay taxes

There are three ways that tax is collected:

- by **deduction at source** – the person making the payment is either entitled or required to deduct tax when making the payment, so that the person receiving the payment has already lost the tax from it;
- by **transaction taxes** – dealt with at the time of a particular transaction with the items taxed for example when they are sold;
- by **annual taxes** – or other taxes collected over a period, where the amount of tax will depend on, the profits over a period. In these cases taxes have to be collected after the period is over, although there may be some sort of provisional advance payment.

Deducting at source

This method of collecting tax is widely used by both the Inland Revenue and the DSS. The following kinds of income are subject to a requirement or entitlement for the payer to collect tax on their behalf:

- *Earnings from employment* – employers must operate **PAYE** on all taxable earnings, to collect income tax due from the employee, and Class 1 contributions due to the NI Fund from both employer and employee (see Chapter 8). The tax and NI contributions must be worked out and deducted every time payment is made to an employee, so that the employee only receives pay after deductions. The tax and NI contributions collected in this way must be paid to the Revenue within 14 days after the end of each tax month.
- *Bank, building society and other interest* – banks and societies pay interest on all deposits (less than £50,000) after taking off income tax. They pay the tax due direct to the Revenue. This is also true of yearly interest due from the Government, local authorities or companies on bonds and debentures.
- *Company dividends and distributions* – companies strictly do not deduct tax at source from dividends. Instead they pay **ACT** (advance corporation tax) to the Revenue at the same time. In practical terms, this amounts to the same thing from the viewpoint of an individual shareholder, though a company shareholder is protected from tax on dividends. ACT is based on three-month periods, the Revenue being paid at the end of the three-month period the amount of ACT due during that period. Tax is paid at the same time regardless of when during the three months the dividend is paid (see Chapter 6).
- *Covenants and annual payments* – aside from charity covenants, making payments by covenant is far less important since as of 1988 the tax system largely ignores them. The widespread practice of covenanting money to

students has been stopped. Payment to a charity by a
four-year covenant is still a good idea for a business but
is complicated by deduction at source. Most big charities
have standard forms of covenant to use and leaflets
explaining how the tax relief works. If in doubt, contact
the Charities Aid Foundation (see Chapter 4).

Taxes on transactions

The most important of these is VAT. Besides the question of
what is subject to VAT and what is not, watch also when
VAT is collected from customers, paid to suppliers, and
accounted for to the VAT Office. If you monitor this
carefully, it could help your cash flow considerably. In smaller
businesses, it may also improve your cash flow if you are on
the Cash Accounting scheme (see Chapter 10). When
introduced, the annual VAT accounting scheme may help
smaller businesses, although it won't allow you to put off
paying for a year. Instead, you will be asked to pay tax in
ten instalments with the final instalment being used to get the
amount of VAT right for the year.

VAT is, for most businesses, dealt with on a three-monthly
accounts basis, the tax due to the VAT Office being payable
within a month from the end of the three-month period.
There are stiff penalties which will be readily imposed if you
fail to pay at the right time. So do not pay late – it will cost
you a lot more.

Because of the three-monthly periods, it is worthwhile for a
business to try and collect any VAT on outputs earlier rather
than later during the three-month period, with the reverse
applying to VAT paid out on inputs. For instance, if you
have a number of large bills bearing VAT, get them paid at
the beginning of a VAT accounting period, and you can
keep the VAT in a deposit account for a few months before
you pay it over. By contrast, if you are buying an expensive
item, do so near the end of the three-month period and the

gap between paying the VAT and getting it back will be reduced as far as may be.

Is the business accounting on a cash basis? If it is on an earnings basis, you must account for the VAT on the bills you send out, not the cash you collect. If your customers are slow payers, you may be paying out VAT to the VAT Office before getting it from the customer. In these cases smaller businesses should get themselves on to the cash accounting scheme. This will help your cash flow. If you are making a lot of zero-rated supplies, however, and are regularly claiming tax back, you should ask to be put on to a monthly return so you are not out of pocket.

VAT on imports and **customs duty**, has to be paid when the goods are brought in, unless you use a **freeport**. **Excise duties**, such as tobacco tax, are normally paid as the goods on which the duty falls are released from a bonded warehouse for onward sale or supply. This applies whether the goods are imports or domestic products.

The annual taxes

Taxes on profits have to be charged over a period – this applies to income tax, corporation tax, capital gains tax, and NI contributions on the self-employed. Of course, because of PAYE and the other deductions at source, the government gets a lot of this tax when the income is paid but some forms of income are only taxable afterwards.

Trading and professional income and income tax

Tax payable under Schedule D Cases I and II on trading and professional income is payable in two instalments. The first half is due on 1 January in the tax year for which it is payable, and the other half is due on 1 July after that tax year. As this tax is usually based on the **preceding year basis**, this means, for example, that tax for the year 1988–89 will be due on 1 January 1989 and 1 July 1989. This is tax on profits earned in the accounts year ending in 1987–88.

From the point of view of cash-flow you pay tax on these dates and get the benefit of allowances then regardless of when the profits were earned or the allowances gained. It therefore pays to receive income earlier rather than later in the year, but to meet expenditure which qualifies for allowances later rather than earlier. You can in some cases increase or decrease the gap between getting and paying, or spending and paying, by nearly 12 months. In a lot of cases, it's better to spend money near the end of your accounts year, rather than a month later. You get the tax relief a whole year earlier.

Other income tax payments

Basic rate income tax is payable on any other kind of taxable income on 1 January in the tax year for which it is payable. In most cases the tax is based on that years's income (though for special rules about land taxation see Chapter 11).

Higher rate income tax

Payment of tax due at the higher rate of tax (taking account of tax already paid at the basic rate) is due later than the basic rate tax – on 1 December after the tax year for which it is collected. It is payable shortly before the second instalment of tax on trading income, but after payment of any other basic rate tax. Higher rate tax for 1988–89 is therefore due on 1 December 1989.

NI contributions

Class 1 contributions are payable under the PAYE scheme. Class 2 contributions are due weekly, by the Saturday of each week, unless the contributor agrees to pay monthly by direct debit. Class 4 contributions are paid at the same time as the trading income taxation, on 1 January and 1 July.

Capital gains tax

CGT payments by individuals are made at the same time as higher rate income tax – 1 December after the end of the tax year for which the payment is made. It may be of advantage to time sales giving rise to taxable gains early in the tax year, and those giving rise to losses late in the tax year, so as to increase the cash-flow where possible. Two other points to watch on CGT are: to spread capital gains so that you use the annual allowance of tax-free gains. If you do not use this in a year, you cannot carry it forward to the next. Also, if you have made a loss, cash it in so that you cancel out gains. You can do this by selling assets such as shares at their market value, and then buying the equivalent back again – also at market value. If you have made a loss, you can set it off against CGT payable on gains on other sales. As with trading income, it is worth watching what year things occur in.

Corporation tax

As already noted, ACT has to be paid on three-monthly accounts following the period in which a distribution is paid out. The ACT, as its name indicates, is treated as an advance payment of the corporation tax due. Any other tax due (called the **mainstream corporation tax**) is payable nine months after the end of the accounting period of the company for which the tax is being paid. So, if the company uses an annual calendar year, the tax is payable at the end of the following September. For most small companies, however, the ACT will meet all or most of their mainstream corporation tax bill, because ACT is now collected at the same rate as the small companies' rate of corporation tax (see Chapter 6).

Inheritance tax

IHT is payable during the course of winding up the estate of the deceased. In practice, the IHT has to be calculated and paid by the personal representatives of the deceased (or their solicitors) when applying for the formal Grant of Probate or Letters of Administration (that is, the formal court authority to deal with the property left by the person who died). Where tax becomes payable on a gift made within seven years of the death because of the death, the tax is due six months after the end of the month in which the person died.

Paying late: the penalties

Unless there is a dispute as a result of which late payment of tax is approved (see the next chapter), paying tax late is likely to land the taxpayer with a demand for interest on the sums overdue, penalties, or both.

Interest and penalties are not payable on late NI contributions. Instead, the penalty is indirect – the contributor may lose entitlement to benefit which would have arisen if the contributions were paid at the right time.

Interest on late tax

Where a payment of any of the taxes collected by the Inland Revenue – income tax, CT, CGT, IHT – is late, interest is payable by the taxpayer on the amount overdue from the date payment should have been made. The rate of interest is currently 8% compound. This is chargeable both where a bill for tax has not been met, and also where for some reason the Revenue are recovering back tax (for example, they only discover that someone is trading several years after they started). The interest is treated and collected as part of the tax bill, and is not an allowable expense. The Revenue do not usually collect interest of less than £30.

Penalties for late tax

At present there is no interest payable when VAT is paid late (though the rules are being changed to allow for this). Instead, the VAT Office has powers to impose penalties related to the amount of VAT due when tax is paid late. This can be from 5% up to 30%. The message with VAT is clear: act promptly.

Repayment supplements

If you have overpaid tax the authorities must return it and, make a **repayment supplement**. This is interest payable to you on the tax overpaid. It is not payable unless the tax has been overpaid for more than 12 months after the end of the tax year for which it was paid, and only then if it exceeds £25. The interest rate is currently 9%, which is not taxable.

Tax Times – for a business with an accounts year starting 1 July each year
(Key dates for 1988/89)

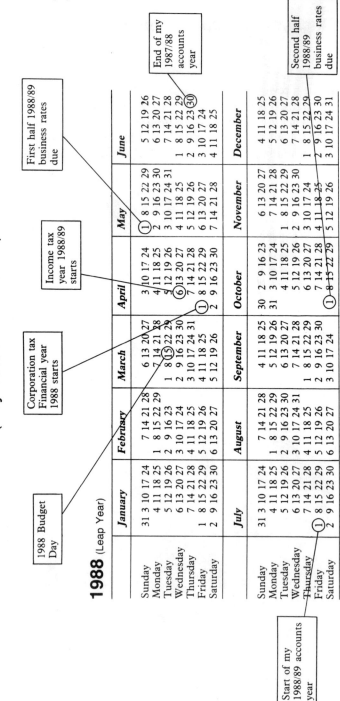

1988 (Leap Year)

	January	February	March	April	May	June
Sunday	31 3 10 17 24	7 14 21 28	6 13 20 27	3 10 17 24	1 8 15 22 29	5 12 19 26
Monday	4 11 18 25	1 8 15 22 29	7 14 21 28	4 11 18 25	2 9 16 23 30	6 13 20 27
Tuesday	5 12 19 26	2 9 16 23	1 8 15 22 29	5 12 19 26	3 10 17 24 31	7 14 21 28
Wednesday	6 13 20 27	3 10 17 24	2 9 16 23 30	6 13 20 27	4 11 18 25	1 8 15 22 29
Thursday	7 14 21 28	4 11 18 25	3 10 17 24 31	7 14 21 28	5 12 19 26	2 9 16 23 30
Friday	1 8 15 22 29	5 12 19 26	4 11 18 25	1 8 15 22 29	6 13 20 27	3 10 17 24
Saturday	2 9 16 23 30	6 13 20 27	5 12 19 26	2 9 16 23 30	7 14 21 28	4 11 18 25

	July	August	September	October	November	December
Sunday	31 3 10 17 24	7 14 21 28	4 11 18 25	30 2 9 16 23	6 13 20 27	4 11 18 25
Monday	4 11 18 25	1 8 15 22 29	5 12 19 26	31 3 10 17 24	7 14 21 28	5 12 19 26
Tuesday	5 12 19 26	2 9 16 23 30	6 13 20 27	4 11 18 25	1 8 15 22 29	6 13 20 27
Wednesday	6 13 20 27	3 10 17 24 31	7 14 21 28	5 12 19 26	2 9 16 23 30	7 14 21 28
Thursday	7 14 21 28	4 11 18 25	1 8 15 22 29	6 13 20 27	3 10 17 24	1 8 15 22 29
Friday	1 8 15 22 29	5 12 19 26	2 9 16 23 30	7 14 21 28	4 11 18 25	2 9 16 23 30
Saturday	2 9 16 23 30	6 13 20 27	3 10 17 24	1 8 15 22 29	5 12 19 26	3 10 17 24 31

Boxes with leader lines:

- 1988 Budget Day
- Corporation tax Financial year 1988 starts
- Income tax year 1988/89 starts
- First half 1988/89 business rates due
- End of my 1987/88 accounts year
- Second half 1988/89 business rates due
- Start of my 1988/89 accounts year

	January	February	March	April	May	June
Sunday	1 8 15 22 29	5 12 19 26	5 12 19 26	30 2 9 16 23	7 14 21 28	4 11 18 25
Monday	2 9 16 23 30	6 13 20 27	6 13 20 27	3 10 17 24	1 8 15 22 29	5 12 19 26
Tuesday	3 10 17 24 31	7 14 21 28	7 14 21 28	4 11 18 25	2 9 16 23 30	6 13 20 27
Wednesday	4 11 18 25	1 8 15 22	1 8 15 22 29	5 12 19 26	3 10 17 24 31	7 14 21 28
Thursday	5 12 19 26	2 9 16 23	2 9 16 23 30	6 13 20 27	4 11 18 25	1 8 15 22 29
Friday	6 13 20 27	3 10 17 24	3 10 17 24 31	7 14 21 28	5 12 19 26	2 9 16 23 30
Saturday	7 14 21 28	4 11 18 25	4 11 18 25	1 8 15 22 29	6 13 20 27	3 10 17 24

	July	August	September	October	November	December
Sunday	30 2 9 16 23	6 13 20 27	3 10 17 24	1 8 15 22 29	5 12 19 26	31 3 10 17 24
Monday	31 3 10 17 24	7 14 21 28	4 11 18 25	2 9 16 23 30	6 13 20 27	4 11 18 25
Tuesday	4 11 18 25	1 8 15 22 29	5 12 19 26	3 10 17 24 31	7 14 21 28	5 12 19 26
Wednesday	5 12 19 26	2 9 16 23 30	6 13 20 27	4 11 18 25	1 8 15 22 29	6 13 20 27
Thursday	6 13 20 27	3 10 17 24 31	7 14 21 28	5 12 19 26	2 9 16 23 30	7 14 21 28
Friday	7 14 21 28	4 11 18 25	1 8 15 22 29	6 13 20 27	3 10 17 24	1 8 15 22 29
Saturday	1 8 15 22 29	5 12 19 26	2 9 16 23 30	7 14 21 28	4 11 18 25	2 9 16 23 30

Annotations:

year 1989/90 starts

PAYE return on employees for 1988/89 due

CGT and higher rate income tax for 1988/89 due

Corporation tax financial year 1989 starts

If my business were a company, tax would now be due on my 1987/88 accounts year

First instalment of 1988/89 income tax and NICs on trading income due (based on my accounts ending 30 June 1987; and other basic rate income tax for 1988/89 due in full

Second instalment of 1988/89 income tax and NICs (see 1 January), start of my 1989/90 accounts year

14 When not to pay

Tut! tut! I hear one or two people saying – fancy telling them not to pay. The rest of you no doubt think this should be the chapter to start with, not to end with. Well . . . it is and it isn't. What we need to do in finishing is to sum up tax planning points made in the book. We also need to look at how the amount of tax is decided in individual cases, and how tax disputes are sorted out.

Tax planning: A summary

There are three key aspects of tax planning which we now need to tie together:

Pay no more tax than you need – If you can take proper and commercially sensible action to cut your tax bill, it is your right to do so. Indeed, you will be expected to do so. Do so *within* the tax laws, taking full advantage of them.

Get your timing right – Watch your cash flow and plan for the effects of tax. If you can so arrange things within the rules that you owe the tax authorities money, rather than them owing it to you, you are entitled to do so.

Don't go over the top – Compared with a few years ago, two aspects of tax planning have fundamentally changed. First, no one tax rate is now over 40%. Gone are the days of crippling tax rates when it was better to do *anything* rather than pay. When planning, get things in proportion. Secondly,

Parliament and the courts have made it a lot harder to get up to 'clever' avoidance tricks to cut tax bills through complex schemes. There are a whole range of complicated provisions designed to reduce the extent to which people can avoid tax in situations where Parliament or the courts have decided that it would be wrong to do so. Here's just one:

Where a tax avoidance scheme involves several stages or steps sorted out in advance, some of which are there just to avoid tax, the courts will simply ignore what has been done, and look at what has gone on behind the scenes. For example, if Al sells shares to Mig, in order that Mig sells them to Zale (rather than Al selling them direct to Zale) the courts may say that this is really a sale straight from Al to Zale if the only reason for Mig getting involved was to avoid tax.

Checklist: Things to think about

- take *all* the taxes into account when planning
- check *when* tax is payable as well as how much
- you now pay the same tax rates on income and on capital gains
- trading accounts need adjusting for tax purposes
- it is for you to show you are entitled to deductions – they aren't granted automatically
- work out if you should trade through a company or direct
- don't just buy – check if you are better off leasing equipment or renting premises
- when selling assets, get your timing right
- pay yourself and your staff in the best way
- claim full reliefs for any losses
- sort VAT out before it sorts you out
- make sure your business plans take full account of your rights to grants and incentives
- don't leave planning for the future to the future. Both for the sake of your business and your family, plan ahead for retirement.

Returns and assessments

The taxfolk rely on accurate and timely information to check everyone is paying the right amounts of tax. To get this information, they have extensive powers to demand **returns**. You are required to make returns each year setting out your full income, so that your income tax bill can be worked out. You will also be involved in other returns: PAYE returns on tax collected from employees, P11D returns on higher-paid staff and directors, returns on any company profits, and on any dividends or interest paid by the company, forms to sort out your NI liability, and VAT returns – plus returns when inheritance tax or stamp duty is payable.

When the returns have been sent in, the taxfolk use them to calculate what tax is due and then issue **assessments** for the tax payable. The formal assessment is a statement of what is due and when it is payable. This is necessary every year to tax trading and professional income and any taxable gains.

We are steadily going over to **self-assessment** in this country. VAT is self-assessed. That means you work out how much tax you owe on the VAT returns, and attach a cheque for that amount to the return. This will come in for corporation tax in 1990 (called **pay and file**). Indirectly it is already working for most people under the PAYE system – as returns are not usually asked for.

Penalties

If a taxpayer fails to make a return when asked, or fails to disclose taxable income or gains to the taxfolk, they have two powers to handle the problem. First, they can impose an **estimated assessment** on the taxpayer. Secondly, they can impose penalties for failing to answer the request for a return.

An **estimated assessment** is the taxfolk's guess at the taxable income or gains for the period. If a trader fails to file a return of trading income, the taxfolk will impose an estimated assessment of the profits of the business on her or him. If an estimated assessment is imposed on you, and you do not appeal, then you have to pay the tax due on that estimate. What happens on an appeal is set out below. It should not surprise if the taxfolk guess high when imposing an estimate, especially if they have already done so before.

The penalty powers can be severe. For failing to make a return, it is £50 in the first instance. For failing to declare tax fully and correctly the maximum penalty is £50 plus the amount of tax lost (twice the amount of tax lost if the taxpayer is suspected of fraud), plus interest. What makes the powers severe is that they can be imposed for *every* year in which tax is underpaid – back to 1936. If a wayward taxpayer has failed, say, to pay £1,000 that should have been paid each year for the last ten years, the tax authorities will not only issue a tax bill for the £10,000, but also penalties up to a maximum of a further £10,000 (or £20,000 if fraud), plus interest on both overdue tax and penalties. That could come to over £35,000.

VAT penalties

These used to involve prosecutions, but have now been altered to be more in line with the Revenue's powers. The Revenue rarely prosecutes offenders if they pay up, whilst the VAT authorities have been much more ready to do so (though Lester Piggott was prosecuted by both). They have powers to impose – and will impose – penalties if your returns are late or do not have the correct amount of VAT attached to them. Again, if the tax has been understated, penalties attach to the demand for back tax. Penalties also apply to failure to register when this should be done – and tax that should have been collected will still be demanded.

Do you have tax appeal?

If you do not agree with an assessment made on you, you
have the right to appeal to an independent appeal tribunal,
but watch two points. It is up to you to prove your appeal,
not the tax authorities. If they impose an estimated
assessment on you, you can only succeed if you can show the
tax appeal body that *on the balance of probabilities* the guess
is wrong. If the Tax Inspector has just made a broad guess,
and you have no records to show he is wrong, his guess will
be upheld.

The second point is that you need to appeal fast. Your right
of appeal against a tax assessment lasts 30 days. You appeal
by writing back to the Tax Inspector or officer who imposed
the assessment on you, objecting to it, and giving an outline
of the reasons. The assessment gives you details. Normally,
both you and the inspector will expect the matter to be
settled. If they have put an estimated assessment on you, and
you produce proper accounts, the correct assessment will be
issued instead. If not, it will go before independent tax appeal
commissioners (or the Value Added Tax Tribunal in the case
of VAT). If your case is going that far, it's probably time to
get the experts in. You can get booklets telling you about
appeals from both the Revenue and the VAT Office.

Past errors: Claim now

We saw that the taxfolk can go back to open previous years'
tax bills if something was left out. You have the same right
if you have forgotten to claim something. If by reason of some
error or mistake of yours in a return (such as not claiming
a deduction for an allowable expense), you have paid too
much tax to the Revenue, give written notice of it to your
Tax Inspector. It can be corrected for a period of up to six

years after the end of the year when the error was made. If something in this book has told you that you should have been claiming for relief, it may not be too late.

What we mean by. . . .

ACT   Advance corporation tax. The tax paid by a company when it makes a dividend. The ACT goes direct to the Revenue, but the taxpayer gets a **tax certificate** for tax paid. The taxpayer can use this to avoid paying any further **basic rate** income tax on the dividend. At the same time, the company can use it to cancel out payment of **mainstream corporation tax**.

Allowable expenses   Expenses allowable for **income tax** or **corporation tax**, consisting of **CGT** expenses of kinds specifically allowed and not prohibited under the rules of each tax.

Anti-avoidance   Anti-avoidance rules are aimed at counteracting **tax avoidance** techniques. They can be broad provisions which have a very powerful effect, such as assuming that someone earned money that he has never received. These provisions are normally only used to counteract transactions which have no reason other than reducing or cutting out paying tax.

Assessment   Formal imposition of tax liability (applies to all taxes); also refers to the forms issued containing the assessment.

Asset   Term used, particularly in **CGT**, for any kind of property whatsoever, ie anything on which cash could be raised.

Assisted Areas   Areas designated by the government where a business can receive **regional selective assistance**.

Balancing allowance (and balancing charge) The adjustment increasing (or decreasing) the amount of **capital allowance** available to a taxpayer when disposing of a capital item on which an allowance has been made.

Basic rate The main rate of income tax (the rate applying to over 90% of taxpayers), as contrasted with the **higher rate** (since 1988 there is only one higher rate) payable on income over a set level.

Benefit in kind Payment to an employee made other than in cash (often called perks), eg company car, cheap loan.

BES The Business Expansion Scheme is a **tax shelter** available for those investing in shares in unquoted UK trading companies allowing deduction of the cost of investment against income tax.

Business rate Tax imposed on the occupation of business properties, payable to the local authority for local services.

Capital For income tax purposes means receipts or expenditures which do not count as **income** or **allowable expenses**. See **capital allowance, CGT**.

Capital allowance A deduction against income tax in respect of **capital** expenditure.

Cash basis Drawing accounts on the basis that entries are only made when cash is received or paid out, not when they are earned.

CGT Capital gains tax – the tax payable by individuals who make a **chargeable gain** on the **disposal** of **assets**.

Chargeable gain That part of a capital gain liable to CGT.

Charging section A section of a **Finance Act** which directly imposes a tax.

Community charge   The poll tax, to be imposed on every individual to finance costs of locally provided services, and payable to the local authority.

Compliance   The description given by accountants to work done to ensure their clients comply with requirements of tax authorities.

Contracted-out   Usually refers to contracted-out occupational pension schemes whose members are not entitled to the earning-related supplement to the retirement pension, and who pay lower contracted-out rates of Class 1 NICs. Also refers to individuals who contract-out using a personal pension plan.

Corporation tax   Tax payable by companies (and certain societies and clubs) on their income and chargeable gains in place of **income tax** and **capital gains tax**.

Covenant   **Gift** made by deed promising annual payments – usually lasting for a minimum of four years (to a charity) or seven (to anyone else) – because otherwise they don't work for tax purposes. Covenants in favour of individuals will not work after 16 March 1988 unless made before then, that is, they make no difference to the tax position of the covenantor or the recipient.

Customs and Excise   The Government Department responsible for collecting customs and excise duties and VAT.

Customs duty   Protective duties imposed by the **European Communities** at their frontiers to protect products made within the Communities from excessive outside competition. Similarly, other states impose customs duties on imports from Community countries including the UK.

DHSS   The Department of Health and Social Security. This was split, in July 1988, into the **DSS** and the Department of Health.

Disposal Technical term in **CGT** for getting rid of an **asset**, whether by sale, gift, exchange or any other means (including losing it).

Double taxation When something either gets caught by two different taxes, or (usually) by taxes of two different countries.

DSS The Department of Social Security which was created in July 1988. This is the department responsible for collecting National Insurance contributions and paying social security benefits.

Earnings basis Drawing up accounts on the basis that entries are made when income is earned and when bills are incurred (compare **cash basis**).

Enterprise allowance Weekly allowance from the Government for those who were unemployed and are starting out in self-employment.

Enterprise Zone Area designated by the Government as eligible for special **tax breaks**.

European Communities The 12 states of the UK together with Belgium, Denmark, France, West Germany, Greece, Ireland, Luxembourg, the Netherlands, Italy, Portugal and Spain. The EC (for short) is the tax authority for **customs duties** and agricultural levies within the 12 member states, rather than the states themselves.

Evasion Illegal measures designed to remove, reduce or postpone the payment of tax.

Excise duties Taxes imposed upon specific goods usually at the production or import stage, particularly tobacco, alcoholic drinks and petrol.

Exempt Prevented from being taxed by a specific rule. For example, an exempt asset for CGT purposes is an asset for which no CGT is due if there is a disposal; the exempt amount is the annual allowance for CGT before tax is payable on gains; an exempt supply for VAT purposes is a supply on which the supplier must not chrage VAT.

Finance Act Name given to the law which each year (sometimes twice) imposes that year's tax rates and changes (eg Finance Act 1988).

Financial year The year from 1 April to 31 March over which corporation tax is imposed and levied, and which is the Government's accounting year.

Freeport One of six areas designated by the Government in which customs duty and VAT do not have to be paid until goods leave the port.

Gain Any realised increase on value on an **asset** for **CGT**, on which the tax will be imposed; more generally any increase in value or wealth (same as **profit**).

Gift Payment (in cash or kind) made to someone else voluntarily without any contract or payment back. Does not count as **income** for income tax purposes unless made by **covenant,** (before 16 March 1988) but may get caught by **inheritance tax** and **CGT**.

Higher paid employee Employee earning £8,500 or more a year, for whom special rules on **benefits in kind** apply.

Income Has several meanings. The widest is anything which comes in, or any increase in a person's wealth over a period, less her or his expenditure. As in **income tax,** it means those kinds of receipt which are taxable under the charging sections of income tax. Contrast **capital**.

Income tax Tax payable by individuals, partners and trusts (but not companies) on some kinds of income (and some things that are not income). What is 'income' for these purposes is nowhere defined. Instead, income tax catches forms of payments received which fall under any one of the separate **charging sections** known as **Schedules** and **Cases**. These are:

Schedule A — tax on rents and other receipts from land and buildings in the UK

Schedule B — doesn't exist any longer

Schedule C — tax on income from Government bonds

Schedule D Case I — tax on trades

Case II — tax on professions and vocations

Case III — tax on interest, annual payments, discounts

Case IV — tax on interest and other income from securities held overseas

Case V — tax on any other form of overseas income aside from overseas earnings from employment or pensions

Case VI — tax on things left out elsewhere such as furnished lettings, occasional earnings of a professional kind (eg from one article in a magazine), and anti-avoidance provisions

Schedule E — Tax on earnings from employments, pensions, and social security payments

Schedule F — Tax on payments from UK companies of dividends and other forms of distribution

Income tax year   The year running from 6 April to 5 April over which income tax is imposed and levied each year.

Indexation allowance   The adjustment to be made to any **allowable expenditure** against a **gain** for **CGT** to reflect the rise in prices between buying the asset and disposing of it.

Industrial buildings   The only buildings (special industries aside) for which **capital allowances** are available.

Inheritance tax   The tax payable on someone's death in connection with property left by that person on his death, or gifts made within seven years before the death, or certain payments made through settlements in that period.

Inland Revenue   See **IRC**. The Government department in charge of our direct taxes: income tax, CGT, corporation tax, stamp duties, inheritance tax.

Input tax   VAT paid by a taxpayer on inputs to the business, that is, supplies made to the taxpayer. Deductible from **output tax**.

Inspector of Taxes   The local representative of the Inland Revenue, responsible for income tax CGT and corporation tax for a district.

IRC   Inland Revenue Commissioners, (or Board of Inland Revenue, which is the same people). There is no minister directly in charge of the Inland Revenue, so the Commissioners are in charge instead.

Loss relief   Method of providing an offset for a loss against taxable income (for income tax or corporation tax) or chargeable gains (for CGT).

Mainstream corporation tax   The **corporation tax** due from a company nine months after the end of any accounting year in respect of the profits of that year.

Moonlighting   Doing a second job of which the tax authorities are not aware.

NIC   National Insurance Contributions – the name usually (but technically incorrectly) given to the contributions payable under the Social Security Acts in respect of the cost of financing the state's pension funds. They are divided into four classes:

> *Class 1* — contributions payable by both employee and
>   employer on the earnings of the employee

Class 2 — flat-rate weekly amount payable by anyone who is self-employed

Class 3 — voluntary flat-rate weekly sum that may be paid by those not required or entitled to pay contributions under Classes 1 or 2.

Class 4 — contributions payable by those traders and professionals paying tax under **income tax Schedule D Cases I and II**

Output tax   VAT imposed on outputs, that is, supplies made by the taxpayer.

PAYE   Pay As You Earn, the scheme under which employers have to collect income tax and Class 1 NICs from employees' pay before it is paid.

P11D   Form used to report non-cash earnings of **higher paid employees** and directors.

Personal allowances   The tax-free amounts granted to all individuals before income tax is levied on a year's **taxable income**.

Personal pension   The scheme for non-state retirement pensions introduced in 1988 which can be purchased (with available income tax relief) by anyone.

Plant and machinery   Official language used to describe business equipment on which **capital allowances** are available.

Post-tax   Looking at something after taking into account the tax payable, (for example, the post-tax cost of a deductible expense is less than it costs you in cash terms).

Preceding year basis   The rule whereby income tax on trading income is normally charged on the income not of the year of charge but of the previous year.

Profit   Has several meanings, as do **gain** and **income**; can mean all receipts from something (gross profits); or all income less expenses (net profits); or revenue receipts liable to income tax (annual profits).

Ratable value   Value put on a property so that anyone occupying it can be charged rates, based on notional annual rental value.

Rates   The tax payable to a local council by anyone occupying land or buildings within the area of the local authority.

Regional selective assistance   Name given to the power of the Department of Trade and Industry, Scottish Office and Welsh Office to issue grants to assist industries create or protect employment in the **assisted areas**.

Rollover relief   Relief from **CGT** when tax due under the tax can be postponed, or rolled over, if the taxpayer carries out some action (eg spending the gain on replacement assets).

Stamp duty   Tax paid for a stamp (usually stamped in the old sense) placed on documents, without which the documents are not fully valid; currently required on most conveyances, leases and transfers of shares.

Standard rate   The main rate of VAT; also the main rate of Class 1 NICs (compare the **Basic rate** of income tax).

Supply   Name given to a transaction on which VAT must be imposed – the transfer of ownership of goods or the rendering of services whether or not for a price.

Tax avoidance   Any legal steps to remove, reduce, or postpone tax payments (as compared with **evasion**).

Tax break   An opportunity to reduce your tax bill – also tax **shelter**, an Americanism used to refer to anything which will shelter your income or capital from tax, ie can be used to offset and reduce your tax bill.

Tax certificate   Or **certificate of deduction,** shows that tax has been deducted at source on a payment, or that ACT has been paid on a dividend; used by the recipient to claim a **tax credit.**

Tax credit   Credit against tax due from a taxpayer because tax has been collected or paid by someone else (eg on a dividend).

Tax haven   A country where tax is levied at a low rate or not at all.

Tax invoice   Invoice or bill that must be issued for VAT purposes by a taxpayer imposing VAT on supplies to another VAT taxpayer.

Tax point   Time when VAT becomes payable on a supply.

Taxable income   That amount of a person's income which is liable to income tax under the **income tax schedules and cases.**

VAT   Value added tax. This is the tax payable when anyone makes a supply of goods or services in the course or furtherance of any economic activity carried on by the supplier, unless it is an **exempt** supply.

Year of assessment   The technical name of the **income tax year.**

Zero-rate   A nil rate of tax – used in VAT to allow a supplier to recover the **input tax** whilst charging no **output tax.**

Forms you may need

Form 41G

Inland Revenue
Income Tax

Reference

SPECIMEN

Dear Sir/Madam

I understand that you are now in business on your own account or subcontracting in the Construction Industry and I shall be obliged if you will let me have the information asked for below and overleaf as soon as possible.

If this is the first time you have been in business on your own account a booklet IR28 entitled "Starting in Business" is available on request to help explain your tax position. If there are any further income tax points on which you are in doubt you may like to call here. If so, I shall be pleased to arrange an appointment.

National Insurance Contributions (Class 2) are normally payable when you become self employed and you should contact your local DHSS Office about this.

Yours faithfully,

District date stamp

H.M. Inspector of Taxes

Enquiries about yourself and any business partners

Yourself

Your surname	
Your first names	
Your private address	
	Postcode

Tax Office to which last
Income Tax Return made *

Reference in that Office *

National Insurance Number

Date of birth

* If you are a married woman the answers to these questions should relate to the husband.

Business partners

	Partner 1	Partner 2	Partner 3
Partner's surname			
Partner's first names			
Partner's private address			
	Postcode	Postcode	Postcode

If you have more than three business partners please give the names and addresses of any other partners on a separate sheet

41G(1987)

Please turn over

Enquiries about the business	Replies

1. In what name is the business carried on, if not in your own name?

1.

2. What is the business address, including postcode, if different from your private address?

2.

Postcode

3. What is the nature of the business?

3.

4. When did you start in this business?

4. 19

5. If you took over an existing business, from whom did you acquire it?

5. Name

Address

Postcode

6. To what date do you propose to make up your business accounts?

If they are to be prepared by an accountant, please give his name and address including postcode.

6. 19

Name

Address

Postcode

SPECIMEN

7. If you are not already operating PAYE as an employer, have you any employees earning
   - more than £45.00 a week or £195 a month?
   - more than £1 a week who have other employment?

7. Yes   No

Please '/' appropriate box.

Personal enquiries	Replies

8. Were you employed or were you self employed before you started this business?

What was the name and address of the business or employer. Please provide this information even if you had a period of unemployment between leaving employment and starting your own business.

If you still have the leaving certificate form P45 handed to you by your last employer, please attach it and give the leaving date.

8. Employed   Self employed   '/' one box

Name

Address

Postcode

Date of leaving shown on P45   19

9. If this is your first occupation since leaving full time education on what date did the education cease?

9. Date education ceased   19

10. If in addition to running your business you are in paid employment, or are continuing an existing business, please give the name and address of the employer/existing business.

10. Name

Address

Is this an existing business or employment?

Existing business   Employment   '/' one box

If you are a woman state whether single, maried, widowed, separated or divorced.

If you are married, please give your husband's first names

Signature

Date   19

Form VAT 1

VALUE ADDED TAX

Application for Registration

HM Customs and Excise

SPECIMEN

You should open up this form and read the notes before you answer these questions. Please write clearly in ink.

For official use

Date of receipt

Local office code and registration number

Name

Trade name

Taxable turnover

				D	M	Y	Stagger	Status
E								
D								
R								

| Rept. | Vol. | Oversize name address | Computer user | Group Div. | Intg | Overseas |

Bn

Applicant and business

1 Full name

2 Trading name

3 Address

Phone no.

Postcode

4 Status of business

Limited company □   Company incorporation certificate no. [＿＿＿＿] and date day [＿] month [＿] year 19[＿]

Sole proprietor □   Partnership □   Other-specify [＿＿＿＿＿＿]

5 Business activity [＿＿＿＿＿＿]   Trade classification [＿＿＿]

6 Computer user □

Repayments of VAT

7 □   Bank sorting code and account no. [＿＿] [＿＿]   National Girobank account no. [＿＿]

please continue overleaf ⟶

Compulsory registrations

8 Date of first taxable supply

day month year

19

Value of taxable supplies in the 12 months from that date. £

9 Date from which you have to be registered

day month year

19

10 Exemption from compulsory registration

expected value of zero-rated supplies in the next 12 months   £

Other types of registration

11 Taxable supplies below registration limits

value of taxable supplies in the last 12 months   £

12 No taxable supplies made yet

(a) expected annual value of taxable supplies   £

(b) expected date of first taxable supply

day month year

19

SPECIMEN

Business changes and transfers

13 Business transferred as a going concern

(a) date of transfer or change of legal status

day month year

19

(b) name of previous owner

(c) previous VAT registration number (if known)

14 Transfer of VAT registration number

Related businesses

15 Other VAT registrations   Yes   No

Declaration – You must complete this declaration.

16 I

(Full name in BLOCK LETTERS)

declare that all the entered details and information in any accompanying documents are correct and complete.

Signature   Date

Proprietor   Partner   Director   Company Secretary   Authorised Official   Trustee

For official use

Registration	Obligatory	Exemption	Voluntary	Intending	Transfer of Regn. no.
Approved — Initial Date					
Refused — Initial Date					
Form Issued — Initial Date	VAT 9/ Other	VAT 8	VAT 7	Letter	Approval Letter

VALUE ADDED TAX

Application for Registration

The registration booklet *Should I be registered for VAT?* will help you decide whether you should register. If, having read this booklet, you decide that you have to register you must fill in this form.

Don't delay in returning this form. There are penalties for failing to notify promptly once you are liable to be registered. You may also have to account for VAT which you haven't collected and which you may not be able to recover from your customers.

If you will be importing goods you will need a Trader's Unique Reference Number(TURN) – details are in Notice 702:*Imports and Warehoused goods* available from local VAT offices.

Remember, if you need more help or advice your local VAT office is always ready to help. You will find the address in the phone book under "Customs and Excise".

Notes to the form

Applicant and business

1

If the application is from a:

- sole proprietor – give your title (eg Mr) followed by your first name(s) and surname
- company – give the company name
- partnership – give the firm's name. If there is none, give the full names of all the partners. You must also fill in a Form VAT 2.

Please start at the beginning of each line, use block letters and leave a space between words. For example:

| M R | M A R K | J O H N | S M I T H | |

Remember:

- it is the person not the business that is registered for VAT
- a person can be a sole proprietor, partnership, limited company, club or association or charity
- registration covers all the business activities of the registered person – no matter how varied these activities are.

2

Show the trading name of your business if it is different from the name you gave at Question 1.

3

This should be the place where orders are received and dealt with and the day to day business activities carried on or managed. Don't forget to show the postcode and phone number where you can be contacted.

SPECIMEN

4

Tick the appropriate box. If the business is a limited company you should also give the number and date shown on the Certificate of Incorporation.

5

Give a brief description of your main business activity and put the trade classification code number which best fits it. A list of business activities and their codes is given in the booklet *VAT Trade Classifications* (VAT 41).

6

Tick the box if any part of your records or accounts affecting your VAT returns will be prepared by computer.

Repayments of VAT

7

If you expect regular repayments of VAT from Customs and Excise **because the VAT on your sales will normally be less than the VAT on your purchases** you should:

- tick the box; and
- give either your bank sorting code and account number **or** National Girobank account number.

Compulsory registrations

8 Give the date on which you made your first taxable supply of goods or services to a customer. Then give the total value of taxable supplies that you have made, or expect to make, in the 12 months from that date.

If your taxable supplies are below the compulsory registration limits, leave these boxes blank and go on to Question 11. If you have not made a taxable supply, leave these boxes blank and go on to Question 12.

You will find more about taxable supplies in paragraphs 2 and 3 of the registration booklet. Normally the value of your taxable supplies will be your total turnover. If you are unsure about whether or not to include some items – such as donations or grants – please check with your local VAT office.

9 **You must answer this question even if you are applying for exemption under Question 10.**

You should read paragraph 6 of the registration booklet before you answer this question. If you decide that you have to register, give the date from which you have to be registered. If you wish to register from a date earlier than you have to, please enclose a letter explaining why and from what date.

10 You can apply for exemption from registration if you would not normally be liable to pay VAT to Customs and Excise because your taxable supplies are wholly or mainly zero-rated. If you want to apply for exemption from registration, you should:

- tick the box; **and**
- give the value of the zero-rated supplies you expect to make in the next 12 months.

Paragraph 7 of the registration booklet tells you more about this.

Please make sure that you have also answered Question 9.

Other types of registration

11 Paragraph 8 of the registration booklet explains when you can apply for registration if the value of your taxable supplies is below the registration limits. If, having read this, you decide to apply, you should:

- tick the box;
- give the value of your taxable supplies in the last twelve months; **and**
- enclose a letter explaining why you want to be registered and from what date.

12 Paragraph 9 of the registration booklet explains when you can apply for registration if you are not yet making taxable supplies but intend to do so in the future. If, having read this, you decide to apply, you should:

- tick the box;
- give the annual value of taxable supplies you expect to make;
- give the approximate date when you expect to make your first taxable supply;
- enclose supporting evidence to show that you intend to make taxable supplies by that date; **and**
- enclose a letter giving the date from which you want to be registered.

SPECIMEN

Business changes and transfers

If you are answering Questions 13 and 14, you should read the leaflet *Transfer of a business as a going concern*, because of the special VAT rules which apply.

13 If you are taking a business over as a going concern, or changing the legal status of your existing business, for example from sole proprietor to partnership, you should:
- tick the box; **and**
- answer questions (a), (b) and (c).

14 Tick the box if you wish to retain the existing registration number of the business.

Related businesses

15 If, during the last twelve months, you have been (or now are) an officer (for example, director, company secretary), sole proprietor or partner of any VAT registered business, you should:
- tick the YES box; **and**
- enclose a letter giving the name(s) of the business(es) and the VAT registration number(s).

If, during the last twelve months, you have not been an officer (for example, director, company secretary), sole proprietor or partner of any VAT registered business, please tick the NO box.

Declaration

16 Only the person specified below should sign the declaration and tick the appropriate box:

- for a sole proprietor – the sole proprietor
- for a partnership – a partner
- for a company incorporated under the UK Companies Act – a director or the company secretary
- for a public corporation or nationalised body, or a local authority, or any other corporation – an authorised official
- for an unincorporated association – an authorised official
- for a trust – the trustee(s)
- for an overseas company, non-resident person or firm – see the leaflet *Overseas traders and United Kingdom VAT*.

Please remember, you must send the completed form(s), with any extra information requested, to the VAT office nearest your principal place of business.

Form CF 10

Application for exception from liability for Class 2 contributions

You should read the attached leaflet NI 27A before filling in this form. Ask at the Social Security office if you need more information.

Surname: (BLOCK CAPITALS) Mr/Mrs/Miss/Ms _____

Other names: (BLOCK CAPITALS) _____

Date of birth: _____ day _____ month _____ year _____

Full address: _____

_____ Postcode _____ Telephone _____

Business address (if different from above): _____

_____ Postcode _____ Telephone _____

National Insurance Number | | | | | | |

When did your present self-employment begin?

What is your occupation when self-employed?

If you have more than one such occupation, give details of each.

What are your expected net earnings from self-employment for the year beginning 6 April 1988?

COMPLETE **EITHER** SECTION A **OR** SECTION B **AND** COMPLETE THE DECLARATION

Section A: Complete this section if your self-employment is more than a spare-time activity or is your only source of income.

Part 1: Complete in all cases.

Do you want a card on which to pay contributions voluntarily? Answer YES or NO (Leaflet NI 42 gives details).

Part 2: Complete if you have been self-employed for less than 12 months.

Have you read the section headed 'Newly self-employed' on page 4 of this leaflet? Answer YES or NO.

Now complete the declaration on the back of this form.

Part 3: Complete if you have been self-employed for more than 12 months. The information you give will be treated as confidential.

What is the last tax or accounting year for which you have earnings figures? From _____ to _____ (enter dates).

In that period, what were your total earnings after deductions?
(See page 4 of this leaflet for how to work out your earnings.) £ _____

NOTE: To support your application you must send in with this form your tax papers or a copy of your accounts or, if you have neither, some other evidence of your earnings (see page 4 of this leaflet). If the accounts are with your accountant or some other person and you agree to the DHSS asking him or her to produce them, give his or her name and address below.

Name _____

Address _____

_____ Postcode _____ Telephone _____

Now complete the declaration on the back of this form.

Section B: Complete this section if you have earnings from spare-time self-employment.

If you work for one or more employers for your livelihood and your self-employment is only a spare-time activity, please give estimates for the year beginning 6 April 1988.

Earnings from employment   *£ _____

Name of employer _____

Earnings from employment   *£ _____

Name of employer _____

*(If more than £15860 put "over £15860")
(If you have more than two employers give details on a separate sheet of paper)
Now complete the declaration below.

Declaration

I have read leaflet NI 27A and declare that the information given on this form is true and complete to the best of my knowledge and belief.

I enclose (a) my contribution card □*
         (b) my income tax papers □* or last year's accounts □*
         (c) my certificate of small earnings exception □*
         *(tick as necessary)

Signature _____ Date _____

Tear off the form and send it to your Social Security office. Keep the leaflet for reference.

FOR OFFICIAL USE

	From	To	Checked (Supervisor)	CF400 to Records	Date	Initials	LO Serial No.
Self-employment disregarded. (DL/CC 12 issued)							
SEE allowed (CF 17 issued) Leaflet NI 42 issued							
Card impounded FF69 issued							
Application rejected DL/CC 13 issued							
SEE cancelled							
Cont. card issued f.s.f.							
Renewal of SEE CF 891 & NI 27A issued							
Reminder (CF 892) issued							
NOTE TPR							
Application not renewed Cont. card issued f.s.f.							

Form CF 11

Application to pay self-employed NI (National Insurance) contributions

Do you think that you are self employed?
People who are self-employed can usually agree with these statements

▶ I run my own business

▶ I risk my own money in the business

▶ I take the losses as well as the profits

▶ I expect to pay income tax direct to Inland Revenue
(This is called Schedule D)

If you think that you are self-employed

Fill in this form to start paying Class 2 NI (National Insurance) contributions. These are contributions that self-employed people have to pay.

If you cannot agree with any of the statements at the start of this form

Do not fill in this form. Ask your local Social Security office for advice about what contributions you should be paying. Their address is in the phone book under HEALTH AND SOCIAL SECURITY, Dept of or under Social Security.

Where to get more information about NI
We have sent you with this form any leaflets that we think may help you.

We have ticked the leaflets that we have sent you

leaflet NI 41 about self-employment ☐

leaflet NI 27A about small earnings ☐

leaflet NI 255 about paying by direct debit ☐

leaflet NI 1 about married women ☐

leaflet NI 51 about widows ☐

If your earnings are low

You may not have to pay contributions. You can apply for a certificate that says you do not have to pay because your earnings are low.

Leaflet NI 27A, 'People with small earnings from self-employment' tells you more. There is a form in the leaflet that you can use to apply for a certificate. If you want to apply, fill in the form in the leaflet and send it in with this form, which you should leave blank.

1 About you

Surname

Title

Other names

NI number — Letters Numbers Letter

Address and postcode

Postcode

Phone number

Date of birth / /

Any other surnames you have used

Please turn over ▶

2 About the self-employed work that you do

Please tell us about the self-employed work that you are doing now or that you are about to start

When did you start being self-employed or when will you start?

[/ /]

What self-employed work do you do?

[ ]

Do you do or will you do all of your work or most of your work for one person or one firm?

No ☐
Yes ☐ What is the name and address of the person or the firm you do work for?

Name	
Address	
	Postcode

Is your business address different from your home address?

No ☐
Yes ☐ What is the name address and phone number of your business?

Name	
Address	
	Postcode
Phone number	

SPECIMEN

What is your position in the business? This could be something like owner or partner

[ ]

Were you working before you started to be self-employed?

No ☐
Yes ☐ What was your job?

[ ]

What is the name and address of your last employer?

Name	
Address	
	Postcode

When did you work for this employer?

Started [/ /]

Ended [/ /]

3 How to pay your contributions

There are 2 ways that you can pay contributions

Stamping a contribution card
You have to buy a stamp every week from the Post Office and stick it on the card.
At the end of each tax year, in April, you take or send the card to your local Social Security office. They will give you or send you a new card to stamp.

Paying by direct debit
The money is taken automatically from your bank account or National Girobank account once a month. Leaflet NI255, 'Direct debit - the easy way to pay', tells you more. There is a form in the leaflet that you should fill in now and send with this form if you want to start paying your contributions this way.

Please tell us how you want to pay contributions

Direct debit from a bank account or National Girobank account ☐

Stamping a contribution card ☐

4 Benefits that you cannot get

The self-employed contributions that you pay may help you to qualify for some NI benefits in the future.
But self-employed (Class 2) contributions **cannot** help you to qualify for these benefits

▶ Unemployment Benefit

▶ Industrial Injuries Disablement Benefit

▶ The earnings-related part of Invalidity Benefit

▶ The earnings-related part of Retirement Pension

▶ The earnings-related part of Widow's Benefit

5 What to send with this form

We need to see some proof of your NI number to make sure that the contributions you pay go to your NI account and not to anyone else's. Please send something with your NI number on it. This could be a payslip, P45, P60, or papers from an employer, DHSS, the Department of Employment or the tax office. Even if you have not got anything to send, you should still send in this form as soon as you can.

6 Declaration

I would like to pay in the way that I have shown.

I am aware that Class 2 contributions cannot help to qualify for the benefits in the list in part 4 of this form

I understand that if I give information that is incorrect or incomplete, action may be taken against me

I declare that the information I have given on this form is correct and complete

This is my application to pay Class 2 contributions as a self-employed person

Signature [ ] Date [/ /]

Please turn over ▶

7   What to do now

Take or send this form to your local Social Security office as soon as you can.
You can get an envelope that does not need a stamp from your nearest Post Office.

Please make sure that you put any papers or forms that we have asked for in the envelope.
We will send your papers back to you as soon as we can.

8   What happens next

If you have chosen to pay by direct debit, we will arrange with your bank or the National Girobank for the money
to be taken automatically from your account once a month. It may be a few weeks before the payments start.
The first payment only may be for more than one month or for less than one month. The payments will carry on
until you want them to stop.

If you have chosen to stamp a card, we will send you a card as soon as we can.

9   Other things you may need to know

▶   **Income tax**
You may have to pay something called Schedule D income tax. If you have not done so already, contact your
local Inspector of Taxes. The phone number and address are in the phone book under INLAND REVENUE.

▶   **Paying extra contributions**
If your profits are more than a set amount, you may have to pay extra contributions called Class 4 contributions.
These are normally collected automatically by Inland Revenue at the same time as your income tax.
Your Tax Office will tell you if you have to pay Class 4 contributions. There is a leaflet NP 18
'Class 4 NI contributions' that tells you more.
You can get this leaflet from any Social Security office.

▶   **Your self-employment**
You have filled in this form because you think that you are self-employed. DHSS will deal with your application,
but this does not mean that DHSS definitely accepts that you are self-employed. If you want a written decision
about your self-employment, get in touch with your local Social Security office and ask for something called
a formal ruling.

Office use

CF1 issued OTOE	☐
FSF	[/ /]
TPR constructed	☐
CF400 sent to NCO	☐
CF351 completed	☐
DD starts from	[/ /]

Initials and date	[/ /]

Endnote

If you have stayed with me this far, you have travelled through a fascinating system which raises and disburses an average of £3,000 each for you, me and everyone else in the land – more like £8,000 from each productive member of the community. That's what it costs to belong to 'Club UK' for a year. That's why it is worth learning about how the subscriptions are collected and how they are spent. Put it this way, if you were told to spend about a third of your life working voluntarily for others, would you not want to know more about it? Well, you already do – we all do. Personally, I want to live in a community that looks after others – and that means a community that levies taxes. But that does not mean that our system – any system – is perfect, or that I need not know about it, or go out of my way to pay more than my fair share.

This book is an attempt to describe an imperfect system, though one that is noticeably better than it was a short while ago. The changes in that system this year presented more than the usual challenge of a taxbook as the system has changed significantly even whilst this book was written.

Help in grappling with those changes and in the work behind this book has come from many people to all of whom I owe thanks for the help and the time they and their organisations spared me – not least in recent months the tax partners and managers at Price Waterhouse and my tax colleagues and students at the University of London – plus the genuine support of both Allied Dunbar and Longman. The text is however mine. Above all (and, as the *Allied Dunbar Money Guide* series shows, this is not the first time I have said this in 1988) again I must thank Thomas, Edward, Richard and, as ever, Lis. *Next* time, I'll get to Skye with you!

The text does its best to describe the law as at the date below. It includes the details of the Budget and Finance Act 1988, and the social security and aid changes that occurred up to that date.

Charlbury, Oxfordshire   David Williams
20 July 1988

Index

Other titles in this series